Steve A. Brown

Leading Me

Leading Me

Eight Practices for a Christian Leader's
Most Important Assignment

Steve A. Brown

CASTLE QUAY BOOKS

LEADING ME: EIGHT PRACTICES FOR A CHRISTIAN LEADER'S MOST IMPORTANT
ASSIGNMENT
Copyright © 2015 Steve A. Brown
All rights reserved
Printed in Canada
International Standard Book Number: 978-1-927355-68-8
ISBN 978-1-927355-69-5 EPUB

American spelling used throughout.

Published by:
Castle Quay Books
19-24 Laguna Pkwy, Lagoon City, Brechin, Ontario, L0K 1B0
Tel: (416) 573-3249
E-mail: info@castlequaybooks.com   www.castlequaybooks.com

Edited by Marina Hofman Willard and Lori MacKay
Cover design by Burst Communication
Printed at Essence Printing, Belleville, Ontario

Scripture quotations marked NIV are taken from the HOLY BIBLE, NEW INTERNA-
TIONAL VERSION ®. Copyright © 1973, 1978, 1984 , 2011 by International Bible Society.
Used by permission of Zondervan Publishing House.

Brown, Steve A., 1970-, author
      Leading me : eight key practices for your most important assignment--
you / Dr. Steve A. Brown.

Issued in print.
ISBN 978-1-927355-68-8 (pbk.).--ISBN978-1-927355-69-5 (epub)

      1. Leadership--Religious aspects--Christianity. 2. Self-actualization
(Psychology)--Religious aspects--Christianity. I. Title.

BV4597.53.L43B76 2015   248.8'8   C2015-900008-4
                                                            C2015-
900009-2

CASTLE QUAY BOOKS

"Absorb the vital wisdom of this book and you'll find yourself leading more like Jesus: less frazzled, more fruitful, less frantic and more fulfilled in the Father's love. You'll experience leading as *grace* rather than as a rat race."

Ken Shigematsu, Pastor of Tenth Church Vancouver and best-selling author of *God in My Everything*

"Profoundly good leaders lead from the inside out. *Leading Me* will help you to look in the mirror and monitor how you are doing on the inside so that your leadership stays effective for the long-term."

Bruce Johnson, President, SIM USA

"I am inspired by Steve, not just by his words on a page, but also his living example of leadership in everyday life. From the inside out, Steve lives this book. What I have seen and experienced on the outside of Steve's life and leadership is clearly the overflow of leading himself well from the inside out. This book will serve us all well if we want to embody humility, grace, intentionality and superb leadership."

John McAuley, President/CEO Muskoka Woods

"Steve has 'hit the nail on the head' with *Leading Me*. Too many leaders today are failing—mostly because of unattended personal lives. This book provides challenges, key disciplines and tools to finish well the race God has set."

Geri Rodman, President, Inter-Varsity Christian Fellowship of Canada

"In *Leading Me*, Steve Brown combines personal experience, leadership excellence and biblical soundness into a helpful guide for today's leaders. Drawing upon years of interaction with North America's most promising up and coming Christian leaders, Steve distills lessons learned into a set of core principles every ministry leader needs to know and practice in order to lead oneself and others effectively."

Dr. Rick Franklin, Executive Director of Ministries, Power to Change

"Very practical and insightful. *Leading Me* takes us through a journey that challenges us to evaluate our priorities and practices. Steve Brown uses his extensive mentoring and training experience to provide an excellent framework to grow in our character, our relationships and our leadership."

Robb Warren, Co-Executive Director, Willow Creek Canada

"A long time ago I was told that Christian Leadership was about 'God's story in our story.' That truth leaps from the writing of Steve Brown in *Leading Me*. He understands that leadership comes from somewhere and its source bears the fruit of the depth of the soul that it leads from. For those thinking of leadership and becoming leaders, Steve's book is a must read."

Gary V. Nelson, Author of *Borderland Churches*, President and Vice Chancellor of Tyndale College & Seminary

"Written from the heart, *Leading Me* cuts right to the heart of leadership—the leader. *Leading Me* not only challenges but also inspires and provides practical wisdom for the leader committed to ongoing growth and development in being the person others will choose to follow. Out of his own experience of Christian faith, ministry and partnership with leaders around the globe, Steve has captured a resonant and required message for leaders as true today as it has ever been in the history of the Church."

Commissioner Floyd J. Tidd, Territorial Commander, The Salvation Army, Australia Southern Territory

"Steve Brown has written a timely and practical book about a one of the greatest needs in leadership today—how to lead oneself. By reminding us that we cannot offer what we have yet to receive or ask others to do what we have not done ourselves, *Leading Me* provides eight essential practices for leading well—by leading oneself first. A great book for young leaders and a welcome reminder to those who want to lead and finish well."

Jim Van Yperen, Founder and President of Metanoia Ministries, a Christian ministry dedicated to restoring broken places in the Church

"In *Leading Me*, Steve Brown has taken leadership development to a new level. In a world filled with tools to help leaders be more successful and have a greater impact, Steve reminds us that we can only lead people as far as we have gone ourselves. While it is full of practical ideas, *Leading Me* goes deeper to shape the heart of a leader."

Kirk Giles, President, Promise Keepers Canada

"In *Leading Me*, Steve Brown has shared a simple but profound learning: to become a truly effective leader, you need to start by focusing on your own heart, character and soul. What makes Steve's message even more compelling is that it's deeply grounded in his faith, his ministry experience and his years of close engagement with hundreds of Christian leaders. The result is a book that inspired me afresh to lead—and live—better."

Michael Messenger, Executive Vice-President, World Vision Canada

"At YFC we have recognized that only healthy leaders build healthy and sustainable chapters and ministries. So we encourage all of our developing leaders to go through the Arrow Leadership Program. In *Leading Me*, Steve has now allowed us all in. Read it slowly. Every other leadership book will only help us in the long run if we lead ourselves first."

Dave Brereton, National Director, Youth for Christ, Canada

"I had thought that leadership was all about leading others. Steve Brown's *Leading Me* opened a whole new approach to leadership. True leadership is about leading from the inside out and leading yourself well. *Leading Me* will give you a fresh approach to your leadership."

Sherry Bailey, Executive Director, Dalit Freedom Network

"Faithfulness: a leader who has lived a Christ-honoring life and finished well. *Leading Me* is a guide toward this goal. By drawing on the experiences of hundreds of developed leaders and offering tangible, workable life practices, Steve Brown gives us a superlative handbook for the greatest of all leadership challenges—leading ourselves!"

Dr. Paul Borthwick, Author, Senior Consultant for Development Associates International

"At the very heart of leadership is the ability to lead oneself. The important contribution my friend Steve Brown is making in *Leading Me* is that he shares what you can do, with God's help, if you actually want to get better at leading yourself. From his life and his experience mentoring hundred of leaders, Steve shares an inventory of actionable key practices every leader should take stock of. *Leading Me* can help us all, from veteran to newbie leaders, improve in how to better lead ourselves."

Rev. Dr. Carson Pue, Author of *Mentoring Leaders: Wisdom for Developing Calling, Character, and Competency* and *Mentoring Wisdom: Living and Leading Well*

"In the midst of a plethora of leadership theories, Steve illuminates with refreshing clarity the most vital element of all—the ability to lead one's self. I'm impressed with the very practical ideas that every leader can begin implementing tomorrow morning!"

Don Simmonds, Chairman, Crossroads Media Group

"In *Leading Me*, Dr. Steve Brown has supplied leaders with a resource that is both personal and practical. This interactive book challenges the reader to truly go deep and explore all aspects of life, not simply the parts that are 'above the waterline.' Steve's transparency in sharing his own journey with self-leadership coupled with his experience committed to training godly leaders will provide you with a wealth of helpful insights."

Major Jim LaBossiere, Divisional Commander, The Salvation Army, Northern New England Division

"In *Leading Me*, Steve Brown tackles every leader's largest challenge, leading the one who 'looks back in the mirror.' This book is built on years of working closely with key leaders from around the world. Steve has helped me through many of these key practices and they have been both challenging and liberating. Profound, practical, God-focused. I would highly recommend reading and even more importantly, using *Leading Me*."

Rev. Dr. David Overholt, Pastor of Church on the Rock and head of Youth and Family Department at Tyndale Seminary

Dedication

To Arrow leaders across North America and around the world
who seek to be led more by, to lead more like
and to lead more to Jesus each and every day.

Table of Contents

Foreword

My father kept on a shelf in the garage a wood crate filled with wonders. It was his catch-all for everything: antique door knobs, spools of every size, springs and coils and latches and hinges and ball bearings and sink traps and all manner of electrical paraphernalia. It was my favorite thing. I couldn't have been happier if I'd been handed a casket of rare jewels. Indeed, what would I do with rare jewels? But this—anything and everything I could ever need was here. Anything I was building or fixing—a bike, go-cart, rocket ship, time machine, bow and arrow, walkie-talkie set—that box had the part.

Only it took some sifting. All those treasures were piled arm's deep and all mixed together. Sometimes, even knowing that the microscopic screw I needed to fix my sunglasses was in there somewhere, I gave up trying.

That's a long and strange way to introduce Dr. Steve Brown's book, *Leading Me*. Except this: imagine a treasure box for leaders, with everything you could possibly need in it and the whole thing beautifully *organized*! That's this book.

It has several features that make it outstanding.

For one, it's all here. Virtually everything you need to figure out how to flourish in your calling—from good health to a deep soul to rich relationships to loving well and ending well and much else besides—is clearly, logically and winsomely laid out in these pages, bolstered with the latest research and illustrated with vivid story-telling.

For another, it's unfailingly practical. Dr. Brown cites a wealth of studies and statistics, but not a bit of it is pedantic or academic. Every chapter, every paragraph, every sentence, every word drives toward a single goal: to help you see yourself clearly and lead yourself effectively.

And for yet another, it's so well told. Dr. Brown is funny, candid, insightful and above all, clear. There is not one phrase in this book that you'll need to read again to try to decipher, though hundreds of phrases you'll want to read again and again, just to savour. (And his stories will make great sermon illustrations and are left right there on the table as though he wants you to steal them.)

And lastly (though I could go on), it's so very honest. The whole thing has the effect of a seasoned combat veteran gathering his troops before a big battle to tell them, lovingly but frankly, the unvarnished truth about what lies ahead and what it's going to take to survive. Dr. Brown pulls no punches and blows no smoke. The man has been there—he's a great leader and he leads leaders—and now he has distilled all his hard-won wisdom into these pages.

Simply put, anyone who reads *Leading Me* and puts its wisdom into practice will go the distance.

I wish I had this book 25 years ago.

I'm grateful I have it now.

And I'm grateful that you have it, too. Well, go on. Open the box. See what wonders are inside. It's better than a casket of rare jewels. Indeed, it might just save your life.

Mark Buchanan
Author of *Your Church is Too Safe*

Introduction

Harold "Bus" Brown was my grandfather. He loved to tell stories. He and my grandmother lived in the same home for more than sixty-five years. Over that time, my grandfather collected a lot of stories and shared them with anyone who would listen. My favorite is about the tree in their backyard.

Each summer during my visit to their home my grandpa would take me to the backyard and tell the story. He would point to a hulking poplar tree that towered over the entire backyard and ask, "You see that tree?" The tree was impossible to miss. I'm not sure how tall it was, but from my perspective as a young boy it was beyond huge. I think that was Grandpa's point.

Then the story began. "When your grandmother and I first moved in, we could have pulled that tree out with just two fingers. Back then it was just a sapling." It was almost impossible for me to imagine that not too long before this great tree had been so small and fragile.

Grandpa would then point out the lumps and bumps that bulged under the grass across the back lawn. Whatever was growing underneath the lawn had even split the pavement across the road from their home. Grandpa would share that these lumps and bumps were actually the tree's roots spreading out, seeking nutrients and providing stability for the tree.

Then he'd point to a big gash about two-thirds of the way up the trunk. At this point he'd tell the story of a big storm a few decades back. Lightning struck the tree and slashed off a giant branch. It astounded me that the tree overcame this attack and just kept rising toward the sky.

Over time this towering tree began to capture my grandmother's concern. She worried that a windstorm would split off one of the tree-sized branches. If that happened, one of the small pre-war homes surrounding their lot would be badly damaged, or worse. Eventually Grandma's worrying caught on in the wider family, and it was agreed that the time had come. The great tree would need to be felled.

An arborist was contracted. A day was set aside. The vehicles arrived, equipped with ladders, saws and ropes. Piece by piece and branch by branch this great tree came down. Slowly but surely, it was cut up and taken away. In fact, it took many pickup truckloads—one family member recalls about 40—to cart away the wood, branches and leaves from this great tree. Over the course of just my grandparents' lifetime, a fragile sapling had grown remarkably, thrived to maturity, prevailed through adversity and left behind a great legacy.

One of the reasons I love this story is because of the spiritual metaphor. I'm quickly drawn to the parable of the sower in Mark 4. This is the story of the farmer who sows the seeds. Some of the seeds fall on the path, some on the rocky places, some amongst the thorns and some on the good soil.

If you are familiar with the story you know that the seed sown on the path was quickly eaten by birds. The seed sown in the rocky places sprang up quickly, but it had shallow roots. It withered in the scorching sun. The seed falling among the thorns grew but was choked by the plants and was unfruitful. Finally, the seed that fell on good soil "came up, grew and produced a crop, some multiplying thirty, some sixty, some a hundred times" (Mark 4:8).

In explaining the parable, Jesus parallels the seed sown on the path to the Word that Satan comes and takes away. The seed with shallow roots scorched in the rocky places represents the Word that, though received with joy, lasts only a short time because of trouble and persecution. The seed choked by the thorns is those overcome by the worries of this life, the deceitfulness of wealth and the desire for other things. Lastly, the seed on the good soil stands for those who "hear the word, accept it, and produce a crop—some thirty, some sixty, some a hundred times what was sown" (Mark 4:20).

The parable of the sower is reality. Like it or not, it is a spiritual truth. Some will not make it to the spiritual sapling stage. Some will get stuck or worse along the way. But some will produce much fruit and leave a great legacy.

Over the last couple of decades I've seen this parable lived out over and over, in hundreds of lives. My heart has been broken when I have watched dear friends, fellow Christ-followers and gifted leaders who seem to have been spiritually snatched, scorched or choked. This list is far too long. Thankfully, I know that God isn't yet done with them—or with me, for that matter.

My heart has also been buoyed and inspired by those who continue to persevere, to grow and to see an exponential harvest of fruit produced in and through their lives. After all, God desires to see us bear much fruit. In teaching about the vine and the branches Jesus said, "This is to my Father's glory, that you bear much fruit, showing yourselves to be my disciples" (John 15:8).

By God's grace and for God's glory, I would like to be a part of this last group. My desire is to live a life that will bear much fruit. My prayer is to finish well. I'd like to grow to maturity, persevere through adversity and leave a legacy of fruitful impact for God's kingdom.

This book has been written to help Christian leaders take practical steps toward this kind of life. However, before you get reading too far along, it's important for me to explain the title, *Leading Me*.

Leading Me is a book about leadership. But it isn't about the type of leadership that most people think about, read about or learn about. Bookshelves buckle under the weight of bestsellers about organizational leadership or team leadership, but *Leading Me* is about a more foundation kind of leadership—personal leadership.

Personal leadership is our first leadership responsibility. First and foremost, this means intentionally partnering with God and others to become the whole person he created and desires us to be. At its core, personal leadership isn't about leading others or guiding organizations. It's a personal focus to nurture a dynamic and intimate relationship with God. It's about cultivating godly character that leads to long-term holiness and health. Personal leadership is also about developing deep, vibrant relationships and fostering the heart, calling and skills for effective impact through service.

For Christian leaders who are often driven to achieve and to do more, a focus on personal leadership can require a major paradigm shift. It means shifting from leadership influence, skills and competence to a whole-person perspective where Christ is central to all that we are. As Robert Clinton writes, "God is quietly, often in unusual ways, trying to get the leader to see that one ministers out what one is. God is concerned with what we are. We want to learn a thousand things because there is so much to learn and to do. But He will teach us one thing, perhaps in a thousand ways: I am forming Christ in you."[1]

Personal leadership is also the prerequisite to all other leadership. To lead others well, you first need to lead yourself well. If you don't lead yourself well, you won't have integrity or be an example to others who look to you for leadership. If your walk doesn't match your talk, others won't trust you. And, in a day when the currency of leadership is trust, if you can't be trusted, it becomes incredibly hard to lead others or to lead an entire organization.

If you don't lead yourself well, you will find yourself distracted, stuck or even consumed by your own foibles and failures. A simple lack of attention and intentionality to your personal leadership will mean that you are not able to fully focus on other things, like the development of others, growing effective teams or guiding an organization. Neglecting your personal leadership can unravel everything. The news provides examples of this reality virtually every day in stories of gifted, talented and experienced team or organizational leaders who are disqualified because of poor personal leadership.

Leading yourself well is an act of stewardship. It also prevents you from becoming a bottleneck and prepares you for future opportunities. If you lead yourself well, other people will take notice and doors will open.

Personal leadership is also a strategic leverage point. You can seek to influence others, but they can choose to ignore, resist or even combat your leadership. You don't have ultimate control of how others respond. But, you do have ultimate control on how you respond.

This doesn't mean that personal leadership is all up to us. We don't have the power or will to change ourselves. Ultimately, God's forming work is *his* work. Jesus is the vine, God is the gardener, and we are the dependent branches. As Jesus says in John 15:5, "If you remain in me and I in you, you will bear much fruit; apart from me you can do nothing." At the same time, our role isn't passive. As we remain in Christ, we are partnering with God's work in and through us.

But this isn't easy. Our biggest leadership challenge actually looks back at us in the mirror every morning. It's us. Dee Hock writes,

> The first and paramount responsibility of anyone who purports to manage is to manage self…It is a complex, unending, incredibly difficult and oft-shunned task. We spend little time and rarely excel at management of self precisely because it is so much more difficult than prescribing and controlling the behavior of others. However, without management of self no one is fit for authority no matter how much they acquire, for the more authority they acquire the more dangerous they become.[2]

There are far too many news reports and stories of called, gifted and trained leaders who implode or cause great harm to others. This usually doesn't happen because of lack of giftedness, education or skills. They implode and wreak havoc because they didn't lead themselves well.

The focus of *Leading Me* is about inviting God and partnering with others to radically transform and practically lead the most important and most challenging person you can lead—yourself. Though I'm assuming that Christian leaders are the primary readers of *Leading Me*, personal leadership is a requirement for everyone. Whoever you are and whatever you do, you are responsible to lead yourself today and every day.

Leading Me is split into two distinct sections. Here is how the book is laid out:

- **Section 1**—Chapter 1 helps you to better understand your unique partnership with God in leading you. Chapter 2 provides a biblical framework of God's design for your life so you have a clear target in mind as well as an evaluative tool.

- **Section 2**—Chapters 3 to 12 focus on eight key practices for leading yourself well. These practices are rooted in Scripture and based on the proven process of the Arrow Leadership Program. If you intentionally focus on these eight areas, you will develop a solid foundation, practical toolkit and user-friendly pathway for leading yourself effectively over the long haul.

One last thought before you continue on. *Leading Me* isn't designed to be read in one sitting. It's intended to be read and processed slowly over time. So, take one chapter at a time and reflect. Make some notes in a journal. The reflection questions at the end of each chapter will help you to process, share and apply your learning on your own or in the context of a mentoring relationship or small group environment.

Reflection Questions

1. Reflect on the story of the tree in the backyard. What stands out to you from the story and metaphor?

2. What words or phrases would you use to describe the kind of impact or legacy you would like to leave?

3. How do you need to grow in your own personal leadership to be a faithful steward in living and leading well?

Section One

Chapter 1

The Starting Place

K ing David's resume was pretty impressive. A gifted musician and poet. A bold and courageous warrior. A skilled strategist. A called, chosen and anointed leader. A man after God's own heart. The list could go on and get much longer.

In this midst of these qualities, skills and gifts, David faced many significant leadership challenges. For starters, there already was a king. Not only was there a king, but Saul was an insecure and unstable king who regularly flew into blind and violent rages against David. He also had David hunted through the wilderness like wild game.

Another leadership challenge was David's team. In the early days, this motley crew must have been quite a handful. In 1 Samuel 22:2, they are described: "all those who were in distress or in debt or discontented gathered around him, and he became their commander. About four hundred men were with him." Not exactly the textbook DNA of a high performance team. In later days, David's military commander, Joab, went rogue and murdered Saul's military commander after he had brokered a peace deal with David. And it's painfully clear that David's own son Absalom rebelled, led a coup and publicly disgraced his father.

Added to these challenges was external opposition. Whether it was facing down a giant, overcoming powerful enemies, or dealing with the taunts of hecklers, David regularly navigated situations of great pressure and difficulty that would stretch virtually any leader to the limits.

Despite this list of significant leadership challenges, I believe David had a much greater and much more personal leadership challenge. At the core of all of these challenges is David's personal leadership. If David hadn't partnered with God in leading himself well, the negative impact to himself, his team and his cause would have been much greater.

David's biggest leadership assignment and leadership challenge was himself. When David had opportunity to kill Saul, he could have done so to the applause of his team. Instead, David found self-control to hold back as well as courage to rebuke his team. In the loneliness of the caves and life on the run, it would have been understandable if he had been overcome by despair. Instead, he persevered in trusting and worshipping God.

When Ziklag was destroyed by fire and the wives and children of David as well as of his men were taken captive, David could have been consumed by his own raw emotions or by the threats of his followers. Instead, he sought out and listened to God for his next steps. When confronted by Nathan, David's pride and sense of self-protection could have rejected the rebuke and led to even greater consequences. Instead, he responded with humility, brokenness and repentance.

David's personal leadership in partnership with God made the difference in each of these situations. But we also know that David had a major lapse in his personal leadership. When other kings were setting off for war, David didn't join his men. We can speculate on the reason for David's choice to stay home, but we know that lust and a sense of entitlement took over when he gazed down on a bathing Bathsheba. David's lapse in personal leadership spiraled into more sin, with deceit and ultimately murder. This failure wasn't about David's giftedness, calling or competency as a first-chair leader. This failure was about David's personal leadership.

The consequences were enormous. It offended God and weighed David down with guilt. The ripple effect left both Uriah and the son of David and Bathsheba dead. It put a dark asterisk beside David's record as a leader. It contributed to calamity within his family, exile from his position and public humiliation as a leader.

David's story is a powerful reminder that how you lead yourself is critical. It's also a clear reminder that personal leadership isn't easy. It's our toughest leadership assignment. It's difficult for a number of reasons. The first is our likeness to sheep. God's people are often labeled as sheep in Scripture. As a shepherd David knew about sheep. He knew that sheep are far from the smartest creatures. They have a pack mentality, and they are creatures of habit who follow the same trail and routine with no desire for change. Left to their own devices, sheep would consume all the food in a pasture and then starve within sight of another pasture. They are easily frightened. They are fairly helpless and can't even right themselves if they fall over.

Despite all our education and advances over time, we are a lot like sheep. We often struggle to make wise choices, we are easily consumed by fear, we get stuck in ruts and routines that are unhealthy, and we have difficulty seeing beyond our immediate circumstances. Just like sheep need a shepherd, our desperate need is for the shepherd of Psalm 23. The shepherd who serves, leads, guides, restores, provides, protects and blesses.

A second reason why we are our toughest leadership assignment is the battle within. The apostle Paul was an unparalleled pioneer and bold missionary leader who saw God bring great growth through his service. In the process Paul faced extreme opposition and overwhelming obstacles as a leader. But Paul's greatest leadership challenge wasn't his team, who had nearly all deserted him by the end of his life. Paul's greatest leadership challenge was himself. In Romans 7:21–24 he writes,

> So I find this law at work: Although I want to do good, evil is right there with me. For in my inner being I delight in God's law; but I see another law at work in me, waging war against the law of my mind and making me a prisoner of the law of sin at work within me. What a wretched man I am! Who will rescue me from this body that is subject to death?

Can you relate to Paul's struggle? I sure can. I can relate to a war in my mind and feeling like a prisoner to the law of sin at work within. I've felt stuck and have struggled to overcome personal battles. I've been puzzled, trying to figure out how I can routinely lead others with a reasonable level of skill and solve fairly complex organizational problems, yet I can't seem to break free from or solve personal issues. Paul goes on in Romans 8 to share God's solution to his and our problem, but the battle and challenge within is clear.

Added to this war within is another battle. A battled waged externally. As Paul writes in Ephesians 6:12, "For our struggle is not against flesh and blood, but against the rulers, against the authorities, against the powers of this dark world and against the spiritual forces of evil in the heavenly realms." This verse and Paul's direction to "Therefore put on the full armor of God" (Ephesians 6:13) is a reminder that leading ourselves well isn't hard simply because of the battle within but also because we are targets of a battle from the outside.

Thankfully, we don't need to face these battles on our own. For Christ-followers and Christian leaders, personal leadership is a partnership. It's a partnership that involves God—the Good Shepherd—the individual and the community. Each has a key, unique and indispensable role. In this chapter, we will look at God's role and our role in this special partnership. We will look at the role of community later on in chapter 5, "Keeping Connected."

God's Role

God has the central role in transforming and leading you.

It starts with God's investment. God has more invested in us than we can imagine. Scripture says that we were part of his plan before creation (Ephesians 1:4). Psalm 139 reminds us that God was intimately involved in our creation. Verse 13 says, "For you created my inmost being; you knit me together in my mother's womb."

But God continues to be intimately involved in our lives beyond our creation. Psalm 139 also tells us that God knows "when I sit and when I rise; you perceive my thoughts from afar. You discern my going out and my lying down...Before a word is on my tongue you, LORD, know it completely" (Psalm 139:2–4). David continues and writes, "Where can I flee from your presence?" (Psalm 139:7) and concludes that wherever he goes, God is there.

God's initiative is also plainly evident throughout Scripture. God not only initiated through creation, but he continued to initiate through his plan of redemption. John 3:16–17 is the best known summary of God's initiative: "For God so loved the world that he gave his one and only Son, that whoever believes in him shall not perish but have eternal life. For God did not send his Son into the world to condemn the world, but to save the world through him." His love led to his initiative.

Through the life, death and resurrection of Christ, God's work has accomplished what we could not and cannot. The first chapter of Ephesians provides a great list of what God has already done for Christ-followers. He has blessed us in the heavenly realms; in love he predestined us for adoption, redeemed us, forgave us, lavished us with the riches of his grace, made known to us the mystery of his will, included us in Christ, and marked us with a seal, the promised Holy Spirit. All this is God's initiative, work and accomplishment.

At this point, we can conclude that God is for us. As Paul argues in Romans 8:31–32, "If God is for us, who can be against us? He who did not spare his own Son, but gave him up for us all—how will he not also, along with him, graciously give us all things?" God is on our side. His desire is for our good, and he is still actively engaged in that goal. The grace given through salvation is immediately met by grace for sanctification. We know that "he who began a good work in you will carry it on to completion until the day of Christ Jesus" (Philippians 1:6).

God's grace, his provision and his sanctifying work through the ongoing activity of the Holy Spirit seeks to transform us "into his image with ever-increasing glory, which comes from the Lord, who is the Spirit" (2 Corinthians 3:18). As God seeks to form Christ in us (Galatians 4:19), we see more and more of his life expressed through us. The products of God's transforming work include the fruit of the Spirit (Galatians 5:22–23) as well as spiritual intimacy, godly character, vibrant relationships and contribution through service.

As Cloud and Townsend write in *How People Grow*, "To grow, we need things that we do not have and cannot provide, and we need to have a source of those things who looks favorably upon us and who does things for us for our own good."[1] God is that source, and he is at work for our own good. While individuals and community do have a key role to play, Cloud and Townsend note that "We do not grow because of 'will power' or 'self-effort' but because of God's provision. God offers the help we need (that's grace) and then we have to respond to that provision."[2]

Our Role

While God initiates and provides the core ingredients for change, you and I can't be passive. We are called to take responsibility to join in partnership with what God is doing and desiring to do in our lives. In *God In My Everything*, Ken Shigematsu helps to describe and differentiate between God's role and our role. Ken writes,

> The growth of our spiritual lives is primarily God's work. On our own, we can no more produce the fruit of Christ's character in our lives than we can squeeze pebbles into diamonds (John 15:5). Yet despite our foibles and failures, God calls us to play a role in our transformation. He invites us to "work out our salvation with fear and trembling," precisely because "it is

God who works in [us] to will and to act in order to fulfill his good purpose" (Philippians 2:13–14). Grace, as Dallas Willard observes, is not opposed to effort but to earning. We cannot earn our life with God—it's a gift. But we are to "make every effort to add to [our] faith goodness...knowledge...and love (2 Peter 15–7)."[3]

Our contribution to this partnership is highlighted in 1 Timothy 4:7, where Paul admonishes Timothy to "train yourself to be godly." Paul isn't calling for the fruitless exercise of personal willpower. Paul also isn't advocating a solo effort apart from community. He's calling for Timothy to take personal responsibility for his development and to engage in an intentional systematic approach empowered by God's grace and with the support of community.

Every Christ-follower and Christian leader needs to take responsibility to partner with God in his or her growth, development and transformation. Taking this role seriously is incredibly important, but we need to take it on by God's grace and with God's strength.

Before we move on to exploring eight key practices for leading yourself, it's critical that you don't miss the starting place. The starting place is King David's prayer.

You might expect that David's resume would produce some swagger, pride and independence. Instead, we find one of the great prayers in Scripture. It's found in the psalms—twice, in case we might miss it. Here's the prayer: "But as for me, I am poor and needy; come quickly to me, O God. You are my help and my deliverer; LORD, do not delay" (Psalm 70:5).

When I read this passage, I see three prerequisites for effectively leading myself. The first is humility. David firmly proclaims that he is not a self-made man. Instead, he is both poor and needy. He's a man who desperately needs God's help. The second prerequisite is dependence. David acknowledges that, above all things, God is his help and his deliverer. He chooses to depend on God rather than his own limited strength. The third is trust. David chooses to trust in God. He not only declares God as his help and deliverer, but he trusts in God's coming provision.

In contrast, it's very interesting to look at Saul's posture. His posture is exactly the opposite of David's. Rather than a posture of humility, Saul exudes entitlement. He believes he should be king no matter what. Rather than dependence, Saul tries to independently maintain his reign by attempting to kill David and by being disobedient to God's instructions concerning the Amalekites. Rather than trust, fearfulness is the driving force in Saul's life. This is demonstrated in his paranoia toward David as well as his frantic and at times bizarre attempts to take matters into his own hands.

David's prayer and posture of humility, dependence and trust are the starting place for getting traction on leading ourselves well. We simply can't manufacture any significant or lasting change on our own.

As we look at humility as a starting point for personal leadership, it's interesting to read Jim Collins' work for his groundbreaking book *Good to Great*. He reviewed 1,435 Fortune 500 companies and identified just 11 that achieved sustained greatness, with stock returns at least three times the market's for fifteen years after a major transition period. One common factor for each of these 11 companies was their top leader. Each company had what Collins' calls a "level 5" leader. One of the two core characteristics of a level 5 leader is deep personal humility. In contrast, Collins' notes in two-thirds of the comparison companies "the presence of a gargantuan ego that contributed to the demise or continued demise of the company."[4]

Though some would see David's posture of humility as weakness, it's actually a strength in God's economy. It invites and depends on God rather than self. It brings freedom rather than a burden that is impossible to carry.

Reflection Questions

1. Leading yourself isn't easy. What are your greatest challenges in leading yourself?

2. Consider the following three continuums. The right side represents David's humility, trust and dependence. The left side represents Saul's pride, fear and independence. Mark yourself on each of the three continuums. What steps do you need to take to move more to the right?

Pride ———————————————— Humility

Fear ———————————————— Trust

Independence ———————————————— Dependence

As you begin this journey of *Leading Me*, I encourage you to pray King David's prayer: "But as for me, I am poor and needy; come quickly to me, O God. You are my help and my deliverer; LORD, do not delay" (Psalm 70:5).

Chapter 2

A Dashboard for Life

Imagine that you are already several minutes late as you head to your car. You quickly get settled into the driver's seat, turn the key to start the engine and then shift gears to begin backing up. It's then, from the corner of your eye, that you notice. The low-fuel light is on. You now have a decision to make. You could heed this silent but clear warning and take the time to stop for gas. Or, you could choose to temporarily ignore the warning and test the limits of your gas tank's capacity.

Your car's dashboard is a tremendously helpful tool. When you are driving down the highway, you can't pop the hood and check over the engine. You can't see inside your fuel tank from the driver's seat. Even when parked in your driveway, the complex mix of hundreds of parts, multiple computers, various fluids and pressures are overwhelming to most people. The dashboard solves this problem.

The dashboard identifies the key functions and provides a simple overview at a glance. These few gauges can give you a fairly clear and objective overview of the car's operating condition. Then, whatever your mechanical aptitude, you can have a more objective level of confidence or concern as you drive. If a yellow or red warning light comes on the dashboard, you can make a choice. One choice is to cover it over with duct tape and ignore it. Another choice is to take action to investigate and rectify the potential problem.

The simple concept of a car dashboard can also be applied to your life. By identifying some key indicators of health, a dashboard of gauges can be created to provide a simple, objective system of feedback. While not scientific, a dashboard can be a simple way to keep on track and to watch for emerging problems. It provides helpful feedback and perspective in the midst of everyday life. If you are a Christian leader operating at high speeds with limited feedback and time for reflection, a dashboard can be a particularly helpful tool for leading yourself.

There are many possible dashboard gauges for the Christian life, but there are four specific gauges that emerge as repeated themes from the life of Jesus and throughout Scripture. These four gauges provide a practical tool for self-evaluation, but they also paint a clear target of God's intention for our lives.

Gauge #1—Spiritual Intimacy

In Mark 1:9–11 we are given a beautiful snapshot. It's the story of Jesus' baptism. It provides a unique window into the precious intimacy that Jesus shared with his heavenly Father and the Holy Spirit. Jesus was being baptized by John the Baptist, and as he came up out of the water, "he saw heaven being torn open and the Spirit descending on him like a dove" (Mark 1:10). Then, Jesus heard these words from his father in heaven: "You are my Son, whom I love; with you I am well pleased" (Mark 1:11).

It's critical to note that these public words were shared **before** Jesus began his ministry or accomplished anything. These words were publicly shared to reinforce Jesus' primary identity, position and value as God's deeply loved son.

These very clear, personal and encouraging words also highlight the intimate relationship between Jesus and his Father. As Arrow Leadership's founder Leighton Ford writes, "Like the patriarchs and prophets in the days of old, he (Jesus) was hearing a call. Yet Jesus' call was completely different because it was the affirmation of a special intimacy and identity with God. He and his Father were one—one in nature, in love and in purpose."[1]

The same can be said of Jesus and the Holy Spirit. They, too, were one—in nature, in love and in purpose. The description of the Holy Spirit descending on Jesus is a vivid reminder that Jesus' life was lived in a dynamic, intimate and dependent relationship with the Spirit.

Beyond this one snapshot, the Gospels demonstrate that Jesus sought out, pursued and enjoyed a dynamic and intimate spiritual relationship with the Father throughout his earthly life. A few verses later, in Mark 1:35, we read that "while it was still dark, Jesus got up, left the house and went off to a solitary place, where he prayed." I don't believe that this time with the Father was simply a prerequisite for leading or having a greater impact; it was first about intimacy and relationship.

You are I are also created for an intimate spiritual relationship with God. This is the foundation and wellspring of the Christian life. Os Guinness writes, "Our primary calling as followers of Christ is by him, to him and for him. First and foremost we are called to Someone (God), not to something (such as motherhood, politics or teaching) or to somewhere (such as the inner city or Outer Mongolia)."[2] Too often I've been reminded by this quote that I'm putting the "something" or "somewhere" ahead of my primary calling.

Since intimacy with God is central to our life and to following Christ, the first dashboard gauge is the spiritual intimacy gauge. This is the vertical or "being" dimension of our life. It's about receiving love from God and abiding in, loving, becoming one with and having a friendship with Christ.

At its very core, the spiritual intimacy gauge starts with receiving God's love. It's about grasping "how wide and long and high and deep is the love of Christ, and to know this love that surpasses knowledge— that you may be filled to the measure of all the fullness of God" (Ephesians 3:18–19). Receiving God's love transforms us from the inside out. It determines our great value and shapes our identity.

The spiritual intimacy gauge is also about nurturing this critical relationship. The spiritual disciplines are one key way to cultivate intimacy with God. Our response back to God is one of worship and love—heart, mind and soul.

As the wellspring for the Christian life, our intimacy with God shouldn't turn us inward. Instead, it should overflow to the rest of our life. If we understand and receive God's lavish love for us, then it impacts our character. As Scripture says, "If you love me, keep my commands" (John 14:15). In other words, our love for God will lead to godly choices and actions. Similarly, if we internalize God's love, it will impact our relationships. As Jesus said, "My command is this: Love each other as I have loved you" (John 15:12). Finally, if we understand even a tiny fraction of the magnitude of God's love for us and the entire world, then his love will overflow through us in service to a world in need.

The spiritual intimacy gauge helps you assess how you are doing in cultivating this critical and central area of your life and leadership. To begin to get a reading of this gauge, you can ask yourself some questions. These questions will get you started:

- Is God's love really real for you? Is God's love easy or hard for you to receive and internalize?

- Where do you find your worth? In Christ, in others, or in your title or accomplishments?

- Which of these words and phrases would you use to describe your intimacy with God: dry, distant, neglected, fragile, real, growing, deep, intimate, overflowing?

- Are you intentional about growing with God through disciplined spiritual exercise and rhythms?

- Are you depending on and trusting God more than yourself or other things?

Gauge #2—Character

Immediately following his baptism, Jesus was sent to the desert. In this barren setting after forty long days Jesus was tempted by Satan. This snapshot is just one example of Jesus' ongoing experience of temptation and conflict. As Hebrews 4:15 states, "For we do not have a high priest who is unable to empathize with our weaknesses, but we have one who has been tempted in every way, just as we are—yet he did not sin."

In the midst of this ongoing temptation and conflict, Jesus learned obedience, and his character was formed. Jesus was always perfect, holy and innocent of any wrong before God, but as Hebrews 5:8–9 says, "Son though he was, he learned obedience from what he suffered and, once made perfect, he became the source of eternal salvation for all who obey him." To say this in another way, the virtues of obedience and character were developed in Jesus' life over time.

You and I have another story. We are neither perfect nor innocent before God. We have fallen short in obedient and holiness. Our character has been corrupted, but God desires to change this reality. His aim is to transform us to be like Christ. The grace we received in our salvation is the good work that was begun in us. Ultimately, this good work is carried on to completion by God's grace in the process of our sanctification.

Our character goes deep and wide. In *A Fish Out of Water*, George Barna provides a vivid description of character:

> Character matters. The word *character* is derived from the Greek term that refers to engraving, implying that character is the sum of the indelible marks imprinted on you which shape your thoughts and behavior. Character is your inner substance—the content of your heart that is manifested through your behavior and values. Character in other words, is who you are when nobody's looking. The real you.[3]

As God seeks to transform our character, he is seeking our obedience, holiness and health. He desires that our lives incorporate and represent his godly character. This is for our own good. Godly character protects us and provides for us. Our godly character also illustrates and demonstrates God's character to others.

The fruit of the Spirit give a beautiful picture of God's desire for our character. Our lives are to be marked by "love, joy, peace, forbearance, kindness, goodness, faithfulness, gentleness, and self-control" (Galatians 5:22–23).

For Christian leaders, God desires another layer of character. In 1 Timothy 3:1–13 and Titus 1:5–9 Paul gives his protégé Timothy a list of character qualities for those called to lead the Church. While these qualities are required for elders, overseers and deacons, it can be argued that this list isn't for a few but God's desire for all Christ-followers.

As you read over these lists of qualities for elders, you will notice that something stands out. Actually, it's the absence of something that stands out. It's the near absence of competencies in the lists. The lists are almost exclusively about character.

Character is critically important for leaders because leaders face a special danger. In pointing out this danger, pastor and author Andy Stanley writes, "Your talent and giftedness as a leader has the potential to take you farther than your character can sustain you. That ought to scare you."[4] Instead of relying on talent and giftedness, leaders need to be like icebergs. Though talent and giftedness may be seen at times above the waterline, they are supported underneath the waterline by a great depth of character.

Leaders also need to be positive examples. This means that leaders need to walk the talk. Integrity of character helps others to follow our lead. As Andy Stanley writes, "You can lead without character. But character is what makes you a leader worth following."[5]

The apostle Paul was able to point to his own example in character and integrity repeatedly. To the Corinthians he said, "Follow my example, as I follow the example of Christ" (1 Corinthians 11:1). To Timothy he wrote,

> You, however, know all about my teaching, my way of life, my purpose, faith, patience, love, endurance, persecutions, sufferings...But as for you, continue in what you have learned and have become convinced of, because you know those from whom you learned it. (2 Timothy 3:10–14)

Paul's example and character made him a leader worth following. It made him a safe leader and a trustworthy leader whom others could follow.

God also gives this list of character qualities for leaders because leaders need to be focused on the mission. This requires leading yourself well. If you can't lead yourself, you will be consumed with inner battles and struggles rather than focused on the mission God has given.

The character gauge is about God's transforming work in your character. It's no less spiritual than the spiritual intimacy gauge. As Dallas Willard writes, "The transformation of godly character is a supernatural outflow of the life of Christ in us as expressed through the fruit of the Spirit."[6] It encompasses holiness and obedience (in your thinking and actions). It's about your integrity. If there is integrity, then there is congruency between the person everyone sees publicly and the person you know privately. Character is also intertwined with areas you need to take responsibility for: your emotions, your resiliency, your energy level and your self-care.

The character gauge helps you reflect and evaluate this key dimension of your life. These questions will provide a starting point:

- In reflecting on holiness and obedience, which of these words or phrases would describe you: defeated, stuck, struggling, transforming, pursuing obedience, purity?

- Where isn't there congruency between your public persona and your private life?

- Reflect on the list of the fruit of the Spirit (Galatians 5:22–23). Is your behavior in alignment with these fruit often, sometimes or not so much?

- Read over the list of characteristics in 1 Timothy 3:1–13. Which of these characteristics would others see in you? Where are you struggling?

- Is there an aspect of your character that others shouldn't seek to replicate right now?

Gauge #3—Relational

Soon after Jesus' desert experience, he begins calling disciples into relationship with himself. In Mark 1:16–18, Jesus calls two fisherman, Simon and Andrew, to "Come, follow me." This is one snapshot that illustrates the ongoing theme of relationships and community in Jesus' life.

Jesus' life was filled with relationships. The Gospels provide many vivid snapshots of Jesus with people. He had ongoing relationships with his family and disciples. He loved children, reached out to the sick and marginalized, spent time with the sinful, challenged the religious and engaged the powerful. Jesus lived, loved, served and suffered in the context of close relationships and community.

Similarly, you and I are created for relationships. As the director of Arrow in England, James Lawrence, writes, "We can certainly connect to God 'vertically' through prayer, but to feel his grace completely, we have to open our hearts to the full expression of it 'horizontally' through other people."[7]

As we seek to lead ourselves, we need relationships. We need community. As Christ-followers we are one part of a larger body. We need the support, gifts and accountability of the larger body. We need to foster healthy friendships, love our neighbors, engage in a local church, support the marginalized and be ambassadors who build bridges to those who don't yet follow Jesus. Those who are married need to nurture their marriages and invest in their children.

This isn't easy. Beyond prioritizing relationships, we need specific skills to help to cultivate them. We need to practice the long list of "one anothers" of the New Testament. We need to be able to engage conflict redemptively, to share our faith contagiously, to invite others into our lives, to develop appropriate boundaries and much more.

The relational gauge explores the health of your relationships as well as your relational skillset. Depending on life circumstances, this area can involve a wide variety of relationships, including with a spouse, children, extended family, close friends, neighbors, people without faith in Christ, church family, etc. Here are some key reflection questions for this gauge:

- Review your primary relationships. What words would you use to describe them: disconnected, frustrating, stagnant, supportive, deepening, flourishing?

- Are you able to engage conflict in healthy, redemptive ways?

- Have you recently connected with a good friend?

- How would you describe the system of relational support in your life?

- Do you have many intentional, ongoing relationships with people who don't yet follow Jesus?

Gauge #4—Service

By calling disciples to "Follow me" in community, Jesus had a clear purpose in mind—"and I make you fish for people" (Mark 1:17, NRSV). The calling of his disciples to form a community was very intentional. Quoting Isaiah 61:1–2, Jesus would from this community launch his ministry to "proclaim good news to the poor. He has sent me to proclaim freedom for the prisoners and recovery of sight for the blind, to set the oppressed free, to proclaim the year of the Lord's favor" (Luke 4:18–19).

A core purpose of this community was to share the kingdom of God with the world. So Jesus invested a great majority of his time in training his disciples to prepare them for this service. The goal was for them to be ready to carry on his world-changing mission.

At the heart of Jesus' ministry was service. To do this, Jesus "made himself nothing by taking the very nature of a servant" (Philippians 2:7). There are many snapshots of Jesus modeling servanthood. My favorite is Jesus washing the disciples' feet. Simon Peter was shocked and objected to what seemed like a great indignity to his Lord. Jesus' rebuke was clear: "Unless I wash you, you have no part with me" (John 13:8). As James Lawrence writes, "Neither success nor status defines Christian leaders; service defines a Christian leader."[8]

Jesus deserved and could have commanded being served, but he modeled something radically different. As James and John angled for positions of prominence, Jesus taught them that servanthood is the pathway to greatness (Mark 10:43). He demonstrated surrender and submission as he "humbled himself by becoming obedient to death—even death on a cross!" (Philippians 2:8). In giving his life as a ransom for many (Mark 10:45), Jesus modeled the reality of sacrifice and suffering.

He also sought first and foremost to seek God's splendor. His greatest desire was to glorify the Father. Even as he faced his own death, his prayer was "Father, glorify your name!" (John 12:28). The result was that "God exalted him to the highest place...that at the name of Jesus every knee should bow...and every tongue acknowledge that Jesus Christ is Lord, to the glory of God the Father" (Philippians 2:9–11).

We are not called to serve in order to earn acceptance or favor with God. Service is an outflow and privilege from our position in Christ. We have been created for works of service and to contribute to God's mission. As Paul wrote, "For we are God's handiwork, created in Christ Jesus to do good works" (Ephesians 2:10). This isn't reserved for pastors or missionaries or just when we volunteer at church or in the community. It's for all followers of Christ, regardless of vocation, and it includes the 100-plus waking hours you spend living, working and serving on the frontlines of life Monday to Saturday.

There are many gifts by which God equips us to serve (1 Corinthians 12:4–6). Everyone has a part to play. There are also many ways to serve. Whether it is service to the poor (James 1:27), the lost (Matthew 28:19–20), widows and orphans (James 2:27), brothers and sisters in the body of Christ (1 Thessalonians 2:8), or even our enemies (Matthew 5:43–47), our service is another way to respond to God in worship as we express his kingdom to others.

Whatever your vocation, the service gauge explores your "doing" through external activity and competencies related to serving through your occupation, church, home and community. Some reflection questions for this gauge follow:

- How do you sense you are serving God through your vocation?
- How is Christ's example of servanthood, sacrifice, surrender and submission expressed through your service?
- Are you being a good steward of your time, gifts and talent through your vocation and volunteer roles?
- How are you equipping and mobilizing others for service?

These four gauges are key dimensions in the Christian life. We see these dimensions not only in the life of Christ but also throughout Scripture. For instance, take a look at Exodus 19:5–6. These verses come just ahead of the ten commandments, and they highlight the same four dimensions. The verses read, "Now if you obey me fully and keep my covenant, then out of all nations you will be my treasured possession. Although the whole earth is mine, you will be for me a kingdom of priests and a holy nation."

As God's "treasured possession" we see a special intimacy between God and his people. As a "holy nation" we see God's people as a community set apart. They are set apart for their role or service as a "kingdom of priests." As commentator Frank Gaebelein notes, "The whole nation was to act as mediators of God's grace to the nations of the earth."[9] This role requires the community to be holy, which necessitates godly character.

If you take one more step back to Genesis, pre-fall, you will again see these four dimensions. In the garden, the spiritual intimacy dimension is unhindered, and there is rich intimacy between God and his creation. The character dimension is fully free from the corruption of sin. The relational dimension is completely harmonious. There is no discord between Adam, Eve, God and creation. There is also a service dimension of purposeful contribution. Adam and Eve have a role and purpose in taking care of the garden.

Once sin is unleashed at the fall we see all four dimensions corrupted. Spiritual intimacy with God is broken, character is tainted and corrupted, relationships now have division, and service becomes toil. From this point on, God's desire is to redeem all his creation and all four of these core dimensions. The ten commandments point the way, and the life of Christ provides the way.

These four dimensions offer a blueprint to seeking the life of Christ in our own lives. All four of these dimensions are interrelated. As the following illustration shows, each dimension connects to and impacts each of the others. The wellspring of spiritual intimacy with God should permeate our character and draw us toward obedience, provide the standard and motivation for our relationships and overflow into action through service.

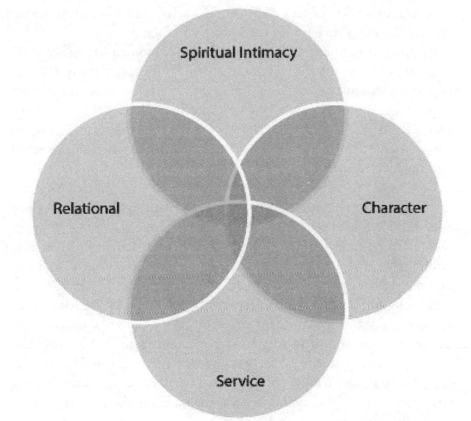

If we remove any one of the dimensions, we get into trouble. We no longer have the full picture of God's desire for us. For example, if character isn't important or is neglected, then our relationships will suffer due to our lack of character. At the same time, character needs the love, grace and power of God from spiritual intimacy and the sharpening from community. Otherwise, character can be driven by legalism.

Similarly, our relationships need to be in the context of holiness, obedience and health, represented by the character gauge. Our service needs to be fuelled by intimacy with God, undertaken with integrity and trust of character and supported through relationships in the body of Christ. All four of these dimensions are critical.

These four gauges provide a simple dashboard for your health as a follower of Christ and a leader. This diagnostic is critical as you seek to lead yourself and to live in the fullness of the life God has designed for you. Your health (or lack of health) in each of these four dimensions will also directly impact your leadership of others.

As you reread about each gauge, take a few moments to prayerfully reflect on your own life and leadership. Process the reflection questions. They aren't exhaustive, but they can give you a sense of health in each dimension. Give each gauge one of three overall readings: *green* for generally healthy and growing (but not perfect), *yellow* as so-so or an early warning sign of concern, and *red* for problematic and needing more immediate attention.

I try to set aside time regularly to review my dashboard. You can incorporate this exercise into your regular Sabbath routine each week or a scheduled personal retreat or simply take a trip to the coffee shop for some reflection time. Using a journal will help you focus your reflection. It will also help you to identify recurring themes and patterns. You can celebrate the positive trends and address the negative.

It's also important to recognize that though God's desire for us is to be "green" on all four gauges, there may be temporary seasons when we need to give added priority to one or more gauges. For instance, God may desire that you grow deeper in character through a time of trial. This trial may temporarily impede your service. In fact, you may need to step back from doing in order to navigate the trial. This isn't necessarily a bad thing. Just know that there may be moments where one or more gauges may be reading a little lower than ideal. Be sure to pay careful attention to ensure that this is a short-term situation and doesn't become permanent.

The discipline of regularly taking a few moments to reflect on these four gauges will help you to lead yourself by bringing you perspective, providing corrective feedback, highlighting cause for celebration and being an early warning system for potential problems.

Reflection Questions

1. This chapter seeks to provide a big picture of God's design for the Christian life in an easy-to-use dashboard format. Take a few minutes to return to each of the four gauges and review the reflection questions. What color (*green* for generally healthy and growing but not perfect, *yellow* as so-so or an early warning sign of concern or *red* for problematic with need for more immediate attention) would you give yourself for each gauge?

2. Reflect on your dashboard gauges. What is your dashboard telling you?

3. What are three to four key next steps that you can take to move toward or stay in green?

4. How could you use these dashboard gauges as an ongoing tool to check in on your health?

Section Two

8 Key Practices for Leading Me

Chapter 3

Key Practice #1

Growing Your Vision

It seemed like a strange assignment. I had just met with my spiritual director. His name is also Steve. A spiritual director is a Christian who is trained to help others cultivate their spiritual life and grow in intimacy with God. We've been meeting every four to six weeks over the last two years. I've really enjoyed Steve's prayerful approach. I've been profoundly challenged by his questions. But this assignment seemed...well...strange.

My spiritual director read a short passage from John 1. John's disciples had caught sight of Jesus. In their excitement, they rushed up to him. Then Jesus asked them, "What do you want?" (John 1:38). He may have asked because he saw them running toward him and was just eager to know what they wanted. Or, being Jesus, he may have been aiming toward starting a much deeper and more profound conversation.

I think John's disciples got tongue-tied. It makes sense. I'm not sure how I would respond either. After all, Jesus has the power to give anything. John's disciples didn't seem to capture this amazing opportunity. Instead of asking for the moon and the stars, they responded, "Rabbi...where are you staying?" (John 1:38).

Scripture says that Jesus invited them to come and see. It also says that "they spent that day with him" (John 1:39). This is where my assignment comes in. My spiritual director asked me to prayerfully reflect on what it would be like to spend a day with Jesus. He gave me some questions to guide me. Questions like, What would you do? What would Jesus be like? What would you be like? What would you talk about? What would he say? How would you answer if Jesus asked you "What do you want?"

I wasn't too sure about this kind of assignment. However, I decided to try it. I set aside an hour. I read the passage several times. I asked God to guide me. Then I waited, listened, reflected and tried to put myself in the place of John's disciples.

What was my experience like? In a word, it was awkward. To be honest, it wasn't so much the assignment. I felt awkward spending time with Jesus. I sensed that he was completely present, fully engaged, very interested and totally unrushed. The problem was...me. I didn't know what to say. I kept thinking we should be "doing" something rather than just hanging out together. I kept looking at my watch, wondering when I could get back to my work.

Then I got to the "what would he say" question. So I asked Jesus if he wanted to say anything to me. I don't usually hear voices, and I'm fairly cautious when I hear other people say "God told me." In this instance, however, I sensed Jesus saying something to me. It was simply "Enjoy me."

I knew what this meant. I believe that Jesus was reminding me that I was designed for relationship with him. He was gently rebuking me for my busyness and my insatiable appetite for doing—particularly doing more leading and more ministry. He was reminding me of God's great love for me. He was calling me from a compulsion of doing to simply being.

Unfortunately, on this lesson I am a slow learner. Since becoming a Christ-follower, my default has been to strive toward more activity, more work and more ministry. Despite the theological truth in my head about God's love for me, I'm much more inclined to show or tell others about God's love for them than to receive it, rest in it or enjoy it myself.

Part of my challenge may be having grown up with a strong work ethic. Part may be how I came to faith. My faith journey wasn't so much about God's great love for me as it was about the evidence behind the faith. The empty tomb and the historical evidence of Jesus' life were and still are a huge cornerstone to my faith. My personality temperament is also geared more toward thinking, and on many days the distance between my head and heart seems a lot longer than eighteen inches.

But there has also been a deeper challenge—my vision. Now, when I say "my vision," I'm not referring to my physical sight. I'm also not using the word "vision" in reference to God's vision for our lives. This kind of vision seeks to discern who God is calling us to be and what he is calling us to do. I'm also not talking about God's vision for the future of his people. For example, God gave a corporate vision to Moses when he said, "So I have come down to rescue them [my people] from the hand of the Egyptians and to bring them up out of that land into a good and spacious land, a land flowing with milk and honey" (Exodus 3:8).

The kind of vision I'm talking about is the kind that is very often completely overlooked. This kind is our vision of God. As Evelyn Underhill said, "The most important thing for you is your vision, your sense of that God whom your work must glorify. The richer, deeper, wider, truer your vision of the Divine Reality, the more real, rich and fruitful your work is going to be."[1]

Everyone has a vision of God and how we see God shapes us. It impacts our thinking and our actions. Though it may be subtle at times, our vision of God profoundly influences how we live and lead. In fact, as A. W. Tozer writes in *The Knowledge of the Holy*, "What comes into our minds when we think about God is the most important thing about us."[2]

During my first residential session in the Arrow Leadership Program, I was asked to make a drawing of how I saw God. Initially, I grimaced at the thought of having to draw anything. I've never been much of an artist. So I chaffed at the impossibility of the assignment. But as I reflected on the primary images and icons that came into mind—and didn't filter them— I discovered three key images.

My first image was a king's crown. This represented God as King, and this is the most biblical of my three images. After all, God is King. He is "King of kings and Lord of lords" (Revelation 19:16). God created, governs and sustains all creation from his heavenly throne. On the surface, there is nothing wrong with this image. Where I got off track was seeing God almost exclusively as King and me almost exclusively as his servant. I hadn't embraced (or even considered) that God is also "Abba" Father and that I am his dearly loved child. My view of God translated into me serving the King without having an intimate relationship with him.

The second image may seem very strange, but I saw God as a shark. Not the kind of shark that lives in the ocean, but a spiritual shark. To be more specific, I saw God as a spiritual loan shark. I knew that through Jesus' life, death and resurrection, the price for my sin had been paid and my debts erased. However, I believed that I needed to pay God back, or at least make interest payments through my good behavior, works and service. I privately worried that if I didn't do enough, I would experience some sort of spiritual shakedown by God. Maybe I had been watching too many crime dramas, but I sensed that God had significant expectations and that I needed to perform well to meet them. Or else.

Lastly, the third image is of God as the giver of gold stars. To explain this one, we need to visit my elementary school classroom. In my early years of elementary school we had a chart on the wall. Our names were listed down the side of the chart, and space was left in columns beside our names. This space was for collecting gold stars.

It worked like this. You got a gold star if and when you finished your work, took it to the teacher for marking and had done it correctly. If you did these three things, you would get a gold star. Then, with gold star in hand, you would race over to the chart and put the star beside your name. If you had lots of gold stars beside your name, this meant that you had consistently finished your work and done it correctly. And, if you had the magic number of gold stars, it was prize time—you got to choose a prize from the teacher's treasure chest.

How do gold stars in elementary school relate to my vision of God? Well, I believed that I needed to earn points with God through my hard and diligent good works. By earning enough points, I could win the prize of God's favor. In other words, if I worked hard and long enough, just maybe God would do something nice for me.

Remember Tozer's statement that "What comes into our minds when we think about God is the most important thing about us"? As promised, my distorted vision of God was impacting my thinking, living and leading. Sometimes subtly and sometimes very noticeably, my view of God was being expressed through my drivenness to perform in order to please him.

I hope your primary mental pictures of God are very different. I hope that you can't relate to the images I have shared. Unfortunately, I have found that far too many Christ-followers and Christian leaders have similar distortions in their vision of God. During my own Arrow experience I discovered that James Lawrence had adapted a model[3] to explain this distorted view of God. In his book *Growing Leaders*,[4] Lawrence outlines what's called the Cycle of Grief.

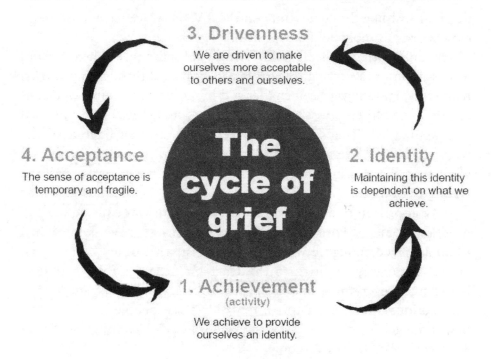

3. Drivenness
We are driven to make ourselves more acceptable to others and ourselves.

The cycle of grief

4. Acceptance
The sense of acceptance is temporary and fragile.

2. Identity
Maintaining this identity is dependent on what we achieve.

1. Achievement
(activity)
We achieve to provide ourselves an identity.

The Cycle of Grief begins with performance. We achieve to provide or earn our identity. Finding, maintaining and proving this identity leads to a drivenness as we seek to earn acceptance from God and others. However, the outcome of our efforts is short-lived, temporary and fragile. If we've done well, it only lasts for a short time. Alternatively, if we haven't done well, it turns into self-condemnation because we have fallen short. Therefore, the only recourse is to start the cycle again and try to achieve more. Around and around we frantically go. The cycle is aptly named the Cycle of Grief because it only produces the grief that comes from great work, without a lasting or fulfilling reward.

I have nicknamed this cycle the "American Idol of Christian Life and Leadership." Just like in the popular music talent show, Christ-followers and Christian leaders often perform in the hopes of achieving acceptance and earning praise—not from a panel of judges but from God. Just like the young singers long to hear any word of praise from the judges, we long to hear a word of praise from God or others who represent him. But, even if we do think or feel we have done well, it is

51

fleeting. Just like the contestants on the TV show, we have to do more next week to simply hold our position.

As a Christian leader, I unknowingly adopted this unhealthy and harmful pattern of trying to earn favor with God through my works. Ironically, I had never been challenged by anyone for living and leading this way. In fact, just the opposite was true. I was often praised and applauded. That's because driven leaders often have a strong work ethic, achieve targets and produce results. After all, that is what they are pouring themselves into. Unfortunately, it's for all the wrong reasons.

My approach to life and ministry leadership was causing me significant problems. For starters, it was exhausting. I never knew when I had achieved enough. I was my own worst critic of my best efforts, and I was overly sensitive to the least bit of critique from others. I evaluated everything and everyone by output. In my short-term transactional thinking, I too often didn't see people as created in God's image. Instead, I simply saw them as vehicles to more output or as obstacles to be overcome.

As a result, my relationship with God was very often mechanical and guilt-ridden. Deep below the surface there was a combination of anger and despair. I could have been one of the church leaders Bill Hybels was referring to when he wrote, "I still meet church leaders all over the world who admit to me privately, in hushed tones, that they have never been able to establish and sustain a close, consistent, vital walk with Jesus."[5] I could talk about a relationship with God, but I didn't really personally know what a relationship with God really was.

Thankfully, I learned that this way is neither the only way nor the right way. There is another cycle in James Lawrence's model. It's called the Cycle of Grace. It begins by receiving and embracing God's unconditional acceptance, based on his grace. As Ephesians 2:4–5 states, "But because of his great love for us, God, who is rich in mercy, made us alive with Christ even when we were dead in transgressions—it is by grace you have been saved." This cycle starts with being rather than doing. It's based on God's work, not our own.

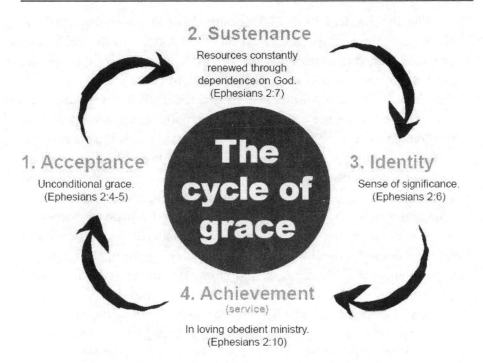

2. Sustenance

Resources constantly
renewed through
dependence on God.
(Ephesians 2:7)

1. Acceptance

Unconditional grace.
(Ephesians 2:4-5)

The cycle of grace

3. Identity

Sense of significance.
(Ephesians 2:6)

4. Achievement
(service)

In loving obedient ministry.
(Ephesians 2:10)

From the starting point of God's acceptance, the next stage in the Cycle of Grace is God's sustenance. We live in dependence on God, not ourselves. God renews our resources based on "the incomparable riches of his grace, expressed in his kindness to us in Christ Jesus" (Ephesians 2:7). We can trust that he will provide what we need as we need it.

Our significance flows out of our position in Christ, knowing that "God raised us up with Christ and seated us with him in the heavenly realms" (Ephesians 2:6)." Our identity in Christ is already established by what God has done. Since it's already established, it's not waiting to be earned.

The natural outflow of the Cycle of Grace in our lives is service. As God's handiwork, we have been "created in Christ Jesus to do good works, which God prepared in advance for us to do" (Ephesians 2:10). Service flows from God's love and acceptance. Service is a response of loving obedience that seeks to glorify God. It doesn't flow from a drivenness that too often leads to personal empire building.

As I reflected on the Cycle of Grace, I saw a very different way of being and serving. I recognized that my drivenness didn't come from

God. The shepherd in Psalm 23 doesn't drive his sheep. Instead, he leads, guides, restores, protects and blesses. I longed to be led by this shepherd. I longed to experience and live in the love, acceptance, peace, freedom, rest and joy that seemed to flow from the Cycle of Grace.

With this new understanding, I desperately wanted to get off the Cycle of Grief and embrace the Cycle of Grace. My first step was repentance. My vision of God was badly distorted. I knew that I needed to confess and turn away from my attempts to try to earn God's favor through my own works and accomplishments. I needed to accept the truth of the cross and begin to live in light of God's great love and lavish grace.

Since this new understanding took hold, I've been on a journey of addressing my distorted view of God and embracing a clearer, richer and fuller view of God. I use the word "journey" very intentionally. I have yet to arrive, but I am in the process, and I am going in the right direction.

My journey has required God's grace, his truth and time. In *Changes That Heal*, Henry Cloud writes that, "Grace is the first ingredient necessary for growing up in the image of God. Grace is unbroken, uninterrupted, unearned relationship."[6] Grace is both God's loving acceptance and his ongoing transforming work in us. Without God's grace, we live in the tyranny of legalism, and we are powerless to change.

Cloud goes on to define truth as "what is real; it describes how things really are. Just as grace is the relational aspect of God's character, truth is the structural aspect of his character. Truth is the skeleton life hangs on."[7] Without God's truth we create room for license of sin. This leads to bondage rather than the freedom that comes from holiness.

Time is the third ingredient in my journey of change. You've likely heard the old riddle "What's the difference between an acorn and an oak tree?" The answer is "Forty years." In other words, time. In my journey, there was a moment of conviction and freedom when I learned about the Cycles of Grief and Grace. Since that moment, God's grace and truth have been transforming me bit by bit over time. My vision of God is aligning more with truth and less with distortions. Though I still sometimes find myself living and leading from the Cycle of Grief, I'm spending more and more time living and leading from the Cycle of Grace.

There have been a number of practices, resources and experiences that have been helpful in my journey toward a clearer vision of God and to living more in the Cycle of Grace. For starters, Henri Nouwen's book *The Return of the Prodigal*[8] has been especially helpful for me in understanding God's grace more deeply. In his research Nouwen travelled to The Hermitage in St. Petersburg, Russia, and spent several days sitting in front of Rembrandt's great 8.5' by 6.5' masterpiece.

Though I had read this parable from Luke 15 many times, Nouwen's writing challenged me to explore the parable from the perspectives of the younger son, the elder son and the father. As I read and studied the portrait myself, I had a new understanding of the profound love of the father. My vision of God became clearer, and I began to personally grasp more and more "how wide and long and high and deep is the love of Christ, and to know this love that surpasses knowledge" (Ephesians 3:18–19).

As a vivid and daily reminder of God's grace and love, I purchased a poster copy of Rembrandt's *The Prodigal*. It hangs by our front door as a physical and visible reminder of God's love and acceptance to me and to all who come and go from our home.

Matt Redman's song "The Father's Song"[9] has been another vision changer in my life. The song is based around Zephaniah 3:17, which says, "The LORD your God is with you, the Mighty Warrior who saves. He will take great delight in you; in his love he will no longer rebuke you, but will rejoice over you with singing." Hearing this song sung as God's blessing over me has helped me to hear and more personally experience the love and delight of the Father for his children.

As I've already shared, I sought out a spiritual director for monthly appointments and established a rhythm of regular monthly spiritual retreats to help me to intentionally tend to my spiritual life and connect more deeply with God.

In seeking to be shaped by God's truth, I have sought to immerse my mind in the truth of who God is and the truth of who I am. I've done this by writing Bible verses highlighting God's character or my identity in Christ on our bathroom mirror in erasable marker. I've done this so that when I looked in the mirror each morning I would be reminded of the truth of who God is and who I am in Christ.

I also began to pray Ephesians 1 with thanksgiving for all that God has done in my life. These great truths include being blessed, chosen, predestined, adopted, included, redeemed, forgiven and "marked in him with a seal, the promised Holy Spirit, who is a deposit guaranteeing our inheritance until the redemption of those who are God's possession" (Ephesians 1:13–14).

God also used my son Luke to teach me some profound lessons about his character. When Luke was a toddler we had a special routine to enjoy breakfast together every morning before I left for work. However, on one particular morning, I had an early appointment at the office, plus I needed to put out the garbage before I left. So, in order to get the garbage out and still be on time for my appointment, I decided that I would break our breakfast routine and let Luke sleep in.

The plan was working. I quietly had breakfast on my own and then tiptoed out of the house without waking Luke. As I was carrying the garbage cans to the curb, I heard the front door open, followed by crying. It was Luke. He had woken up and figured out that I was gone. He was now standing at the front door in tears, wondering why I had left without having breakfast with him.

At the sound of Luke's crying, my heart broke, and I dropped the garbage pails. I ran toward him, picked him up and embraced him. Then I took him into the house, and though it would make me late for my appointment, I made Luke breakfast.

When I eventually made the drive to work, I began to reflect on what had happened. It was as if God was saying, "Steve, you know how you ran to Luke and embraced him when you heard him crying by the front door? Well, your father's heart of love for Luke gives you just a taste of my Father's heart of love for you."

Then, it was as if God was saying, "Steve, you know how Luke woke up this morning? He was longing for his dad. He loves you and just wants to be with you. Well, that's the same longing I wish you would have toward me. Instead, too often, you are focused on getting things done rather than just being with me."

I've taken this time to share my journey with you because in walking alongside hundreds of Christian leaders, I've found that too many have a distorted view of God. They still long to personally experience the love of God that they preach about, teach about, sing about and extend to others. Their personal life mission statements often center around the Great Commandments. Without a doubt, we are called to "'Love the Lord your

God with all your heart and with all your soul and with all your mind.' This is the first and greatest commandment. And the second is like it: 'Love your neighbor as yourself'" (Matthew 22:37–39). But too many Christ-followers and leaders don't follow these commands in context. Their doing of these commands is not an overflow from God's love or acceptance; instead, it's seeking God's love and acceptance.

A clearer view of God puts these commands to love and do in context. The context is that our doing them needs to rooted in first being loved *by* God. We need to respond and act from a view and experience of God as loving father. Brennan Manning powerfully captures this truth. He writes, "My deepest awareness of myself is that I am deeply loved by Jesus Christ and I have done nothing to earn or deserve it."[10]

Leading yourself well needs to flow from a deep wellspring and reservoir of God's love. This is foundational and essential because it directly impacts how you live and lead. If your view of God is distorted and you believe you need to earn God's favor, you are setting yourself up for a continuous experience of the Cycle of Grief. If you are functioning without certainty about God's posture toward you or if you have a misplaced sense that God is terminally disappointed with you, this will flow out of you to others.

This area impacts your entire life. I clearly remember seeing one Christian leader crying as he left a worship and devotional time during the Arrow Leadership Program. When I asked this proven minister and leader what was wrong, he joyfully said, "I am just now beginning to understand God's love for me." That insight is transformational. As this truth sinks into his everyday vision of God, it will also impact the rest of his life. His marriage will be different, his parenting will be different, and his preaching, teaching and leadership will be different.

In his classic book *In the Name of Jesus*, Henri Nouwen reminds Christian leaders that the foundation for healthy, effective leadership is cultivating an intimate relationship with him to know and experience who he truly is. Here's how Nouwen puts it:

> It is not enough for the priests and ministers of the future to be moral people, well trained, eager to help their fellow human being, and able to respond creatively to the burning issues of their time. All of that is very valuable and important, but it is not the heart of Christian leadership. The central question is,

are the leaders of the future truly men and women of God, people with an ardent desire to dwell in God's presence, to listen to God's voice, to look at God's beauty, to touch God's incarnate Word and to taste fully of God's infinite goodness?[11]

What difference would it make if you had a bigger, fuller, clearer vision of God? Tozer argued that it can make a huge difference. In reflecting on the Church, he wrote, "To regain her lost power, the Church must see heaven opened and have a transforming vision of God."[12] That quote should stir every Christian leader to ask, "Do I have a transforming vision of God? Am I sharing it with others?"

At your moving-on or retirement party someday, one of the greatest compliments you can receive is this one: "You've helped me develop a bigger, clearer and fuller vision of God." May your vision of God grow bigger, clearer and fuller. May it transform you and many others!

Reflection Questions

1. If you were given the assignment to "spend a day with Jesus," what do you think he might want to say to you?

2. Does the Cycle of Grief or the Cycle of Grace most describe your current reality?

3. What is your personal leadership challenge in receiving God's love and experiencing the Cycle of Grace?

4. What are two or three next steps for you to grow a bigger, clear and fuller vision of God and live more out of an overflow of God's love?

Chapter 4

Key Practice #2

Unhooking Bungee Cords

Bungee cords come in all kinds of colors and sizes. Like duct tape, bungee cords have numerous uses, and it's always best to have a supply on hand. Though I had used bungee cords for all sorts of things, I had never seen a bungee cord used like this before.

Dr. Carson Pue was leading a module day at an Arrow residential session. He had asked for a volunteer to help with an illustration. When the volunteer got up to the front, Carson pulled out a fairly long bungee cord. He asked the volunteer to face away from him, and then he attached one end of the bungee to the volunteer's belt. Carson then held the bungee cord loosely and asked the volunteer if he felt anything. The volunteer said no. Then things got much more interesting.

Carson asked the volunteer to take a step away from him. As he did, the slack in the bungee cord began to tighten. The volunteer was asked if he was feeling anything now. He said he could feel something tugging lightly but that was all. With some slack still remaining, Carson instructed the volunteer to take another step away. Now the slack was gone and the bungee was pulling at the volunteer's belt. Carson was doing his best to hold on to the stretched cord.

Did the volunteer feel anything now? He sure did. He knew something was holding him back. Not only was the bungee cord holding him back, he was almost completely stuck. If he had tried to take another step forward, there could have been serious consequences. His pants would have been seriously readjusted around his waist or the bungee would have been fired from Carson's hands like a slingshot.

Thankfully for all involved, that was the end of the illustration. The grateful volunteer was asked to back up and then was unhooked from the bungee. He received warm applause as he returned to his seat. But there was a powerful metaphor to the illustration. The metaphor was that all of us have bungee cords attached to us.

Leading yourself well requires you to identify and address bungee cords in your life and leadership. This needs to be an ongoing practice. These bungees may be related to spiritual, emotional, relational or competency issues, and every bungee has a different length. Some you may not even notice initially. But these bungees slow you down and hold you back. And, the farther and longer you go in life and leadership, the tighter the bungees get. You begin to feel their pull, and forward steps become a struggle until you are good and stuck.

The point of the illustration is to begin a conversation around identifying the types of bungees that hold you and me back. There is a long list of possibilities. Some bungees can be more obvious and pronounced. For example, a bungee can be a lack of a particular competency. You try your best and hardest, but results are mediocre; it seems like something is preventing you from moving forward, and stress mounts.

Other bungees can be more subtle. For example, a lack of self-awareness can be a bungee cord. If you don't know how you come across to others, you can put people off without knowing it. Maybe you are unaware of how you have been shaped and wounded through your early years. Remember the old adage "Hurt people hurt people." If you haven't unhooked a bungee of past hurts, you can end up hurting or keeping others away.

Hopefully, these examples give you a deeper sense of what I'm meaning by bungees. Formal 360-degree assessment and informal feedback are two helpful tools to identify potential bungees. When you feel stuck, it is also important to ask yourself if this is the first time or a pattern. If the scenario is the same and only the details are different, this could be a bungee. The good news is that once you identify a bungee, you can begin to address it.

Some bungee cords that hold us back are spiritual. These kinds of bungees can negatively impact our lives, both in our everyday world and in the spiritual realm. Again, the good news is that these bungees can be addressed. In fact, God desires us to be free of bungees. As Hebrews 12:1–2 states, "Therefore, since we are surrounded by such a great cloud of witnesses, let us throw off everything that hinders and the sin that so easily entangles. And let us run with perseverance the race marked out for us, fixing our eyes on Jesus, the pioneer and perfecter of faith."

In his best-selling book *Mentoring Leaders,*[1] Dr. Carson Pue has written extensively on common spiritual blockages for Christian leaders. I'll review and briefly expand on six of these common spiritual bungee cords.

Bungee #1—Unforgiveness

You could see the difference in his face and countenance. An Arrow participant had just dealt with a very difficult bungee in his life—unforgiveness. He had been deeply wounded by a situation in his church. He loved his church, but a number of leaders and people within the church—people he loved—had deeply hurt him over an extended period of time. He had been doing his best to carry on, but the original hurt plus the growing weight of unforgiveness had become a spiritual bungee cord in his life.

Earlier that week we had explored the spiritual bungee of unforgiveness. We looked at several Scripture verses like Matthew 6:15. This verse says, "But if you do not forgive others their sins, your Father will not forgive your sins."

Rather than bringing freedom, unforgiveness imprisons the person who does not or will not forgive. Instead of fostering healing, unforgiveness breeds feelings of anger and bitterness. Just like how an open wound on our body that is not addressed can become infected and cause greater harm, unforgiveness brings infection and causes greater harm.

After some reflection, this leader was convicted. He knew that his unforgiveness was a spiritual bungee that not only was offensive to God but also was holding him back. Though he was fairly successful in covering it over on the outside, it was eating him up inside. He knew he needed to deal with it. He had to make a difficult choice by God's grace to move beyond the sordid circumstances, the complicated details and very real feelings of deep hurt in order to choose to forgive.

At the next scheduled break he went on his own down to the oceanfront. He picked up one of the rocks on the beach as a symbol of how he had been wronged by one of his church members. Then he chose to name the wrong and to forgive the person by name. To symbolize his forgiveness he threw the rock into the ocean, where it disappeared to the bottom. Then he picked up another rock and repeated this process, until he had forgiven each person whom he felt had wronged him in that season of his life and leadership. Finally, he picked up a small boulder. The boulder represented the entire painful situation. He surrendered the whole situation to God and hurled the boulder into the sea.

When he returned from the beach and shared this story, he was different. He actually looked physically different. His countenance had changed. He looked lighter, freer and at greater peace. This outward change was a result of a much deeper change in his spirit. He had identified, addressed and been freed from a significant spiritual bungee in his life.

Bungee #2—Fear

Fear comes in all shapes and sizes. Fear of heights, public speaking, snakes, spiders, the dark, flying and dying are all common. We can all relate to the feeling, power and impact of fear. It's a frequent theme in the Bible. Most of the "big names" in God's story struggled with fear. Even Paul, the great and bold missionary, wrote about "conflicts on the outside, fears within" (2 Corinthians 7:5).

But not all fears are equal. There is a spectrum of fear. On one end of the spectrum there is a healthy or natural fear. This is the fear that is like a warning light. It makes you aware that all is not right. You experience this kind of fear when you wait in line to bungee jump, when you are tempted to make a very wrong choice or when you have to make a big decision.

On the other end of the fear spectrum is a type of fear that is a significant spiritual bungee cord. This kind of fear opposes trust in God. It can paralyze, and it can even take dominion over us. In Christian leaders this kind of fear can lead to great anxiety and worry, a command-and-control approach to leadership, frenetic activity, workaholism or escapism.

Let me share a personal example. A little over a year ago, I was feeling worn down and anxious. In truth, I had been feeling this way for some time. It had been a challenging season of leadership. I knew that some of the feeling was simply a result of the fatigue that comes from pressure, challenges and hard work. But as I reread my journal from the past year, I recognized that these feelings had become an ongoing consistent pattern.

I was tired of feeling this way, and I sensed that something was wrong. I could readily relate to Jesus' words in Matthew 11:28, "Come to me, all you who are weary and burdened, and I will give you rest," but my soul was not at rest. My yoke didn't seem easy nor my burden light. So I invited a wise spiritual mentor into my inner struggle.

After I shared what I was feeling and the ongoing pattern of fatigue, pressure and anxiety, my mentor asked me a simple question. He asked, "Steve, where does trust fit into all this?"

I'm not sure how I initially responded, but I do know that I was mildly angry. In my mind, my mentor didn't seem to understand how hard I was working, how important the work was and how I had to give it 120 percent. I was giving everything I had, plus some, and it seemed that my mentor wanted me to do even more by trusting God more.

After our conversation, the question continued to stir in my spirit. That evening I spent some time reflecting with God about trust. There was no doubt that I was working hard. Hard work was required. But was I really trusting God? My honest answer was "No."

In truth, my hard work ethic was actually a thinly veiled cover for my own fear. My particular brand of fear was the fear of failure. My deep-seated belief was if this endeavor failed, I would be letting down God and many others. I couldn't let that happen. I felt I needed to do whatever I could to avoid it. In practical terms, this meant working by my own strength and getting close to the point of exhaustion. As I worked away in my own strength, I wasn't trusting God. My fear had become a bungee cord.

In response, I confessed my independent spirit and fear to God. I also chose to trust God in this area. When I awoke the next morning, I was still tired from too many hours of work. But I had a new peace. I was trusting God, and I was no longer ruled by fear. The bungee cord was gone.

For Christian leaders, there are some common and specific fears connected to the role of leadership. Fear of failure, fear of rejection, fear of man, and fear of success are just a few. Though the fears vary, they are all bungee cords. Leading yourself well means becoming more aware of these bungees and addressing them sooner rather than later.

Our fear buttons are usually pushed during times of challenge—and leadership is often about leading in the midst of challenge. So how do we live a life of faith in a world of fear?

Here are some best practices:

1. **Rest**—Fear is often magnified when we are weary. Simply getting some deep sleep can bring greater stamina and a renewed perspective.

2. **Identify Your Fears**—Name your fears. By simply identifying and naming them, you bring the fear into the light and break some of the power.

3. **Confess and Choose to Trust**—Confess the specific fear or disbelief to God and ask forgiveness where fear has replaced trust. Then, by God's grace, choose to trust God in that specific area. "By God's strength, I choose to trust you with _____." Pray the aspect of God's character that counters the fear.

4. **Know Your Buttons**—Are there specific situations or people that press your fear buttons? Once you identify your fear buttons, you can be proactive and better prepare. Mark Buchanan, a widely read Christian author and respected leader, is one of our Arrow trainers. He shared that he often repeats a simple prayer ahead of and during situations where he knows his fear button will be pushed. His prayer is, "Fear of _____, leave me. Peace of God, fill me."

5. **Get to the Roots**—Fear can be rooted in disbelief or distortion of God's character, our own lack of skills, limited experience, misinformation, spiritual attack, lack of perspective or past trauma. A trusted mentor, experienced spiritual friend or godly counselor can often be a significant help in addressing the roots.

While fear is common, it shouldn't have dominion over us. The good news is "Some trust in chariots and some in horses, but we trust in the name of the LORD our God" (Psalm 20:7). The hallmark of our lives and leadership needs to be who we trust.

Bungee #3—Idolatry

In some ways idolatry seems like an Old Testament problem. It invokes images of the frightened Israelites worshipping the golden calf or wayward kings setting up Asherah poles. However, idolatry is still a major problem and bungee today. It may take different forms in our culture, but it is still a serious spiritual bungee and an affront to God. At its root is the misplaced worship of and false trust in something we have created and prized rather than God. When we seek our identity, security and hope in something or someone other than God, we are engaging in idolatry. From the ten commandments in Exodus 20:3–6 to the warning in 1 Corinthians 10:14, "Therefore, my dear friends, flee from idolatry," we can know that idolatry is offensive to God and a bungee for us.

Since we are a creative humanity dealing with a deceiving enemy, there are many options and opportunities for idolatry. I'll share just one story from a recent Arrow residential session.

During the final morning of our final residential session, we invite each participant to share a prayer-focus word. The participant's mentor then prays this word or phrase over the leader as a blessing and commissioning.

As I asked one of my leaders for his word, he shared the phrase "pressing on." I began to pray for him and felt prompted to pray Philippians 3:12–14. These verses read,

> Not that I have already obtained all this, or have already arrived at my goal, but I press on to take hold of that for which Christ Jesus took hold of me. Brothers and sisters, I do not consider myself yet to have taken hold of it. But one thing I do: Forgetting what is behind and straining toward what is ahead, I press on toward the goal to win the prize for which God has called me heavenward in Christ Jesus.

After I prayed, we both sat down, and the time of blessing continued. However, a few days later this leader wrote to me and shared that the passage from Philippians had been a highly significant verse in his life for many years. Hearing it again that morning made some significant connections for him. Here's what he shared:

> Sitting in my chair after my blessing I couldn't stop staring at the ring on my right hand. It was given to me when I graduated from university before going to seminary. It was the gold ring presented to the top student leader of the graduating class. I earned that ring during a very dark time in my life. It almost cost me my life. I thought I was wearing it to remind myself of what God had brought me through. In reality it was because I couldn't let go of the things I needed to leave behind. I hadn't taken that ring off in almost twelve years. I couldn't let it go.
>
> That day, however, I took it off. Before getting on the bus to head back to the airport, I went down to the water, and after confessing to God what I was holding on to and asking for his forgiveness and help to let it go, I threw my ring into the lake.
>
> The mark on my finger is still there from the ring, a little indented and a slightly lighter color. It's the mark of what was.

I feel that my heart still has a similar mark on it right now, even though I've turned this over to God. Like my finger, I know those marks will, with time (and God's healing hand), be gone.

The idol for this leader had literally been a ring that he had made the symbol for his identity, significance and accomplishments. Similar to Gollum's obsession with "precious" in *Lord of the Rings*, for him this ring had become a spiritual bungee cord.

Here's one more story about modern-day idolatry from an Arrow leader:

Early on in my Arrow journey, I realized that an undeniable idol of accomplishment resided with prominence in my life. At some point my thinking became twisted and I equated the depth of God's love for me with the significance of my accomplishments for him. I never would have verbalized that, because it is an obvious lie. However, as a result of my Arrow experience, directed prayer and Scripture reading, reflection, and the guidance of wise, caring people God brought into my life, I began to see both the lie and the truth with new clarity.

Evidence of this idol ranged from unhealthy work patterns to unrealistic self-imposed expectations to jealousy of other leaders. Sometimes, instead of celebrating the ways God was working, I looked at other leaders and wondered why they had more responsibility or influence than I did. I was subtly discontent in the calling and work God gave to me. I consistently looked out toward what was next rather than focusing on God's present work. Looking out and ahead is important in leadership, but not without simultaneously looking in to monitor motivations and the condition of one's heart.

Now residing with prominence in my thinking is a healthier God-glorifying sense of gratitude and peace about who I am and the work I do. Jesus says to the Father in John 17, "I have brought you glory on earth by completing the work you gave me to do." I desperately want those words to be an honest assessment of my daily life and, one day, my entire life. None of us brings God glory by completing the work he gave someone else to do. None of us brings God glory by wishing for the work he gave someone else to do, whether we wish for it because it is easier or seemingly more impressive. I simply want to hear from God and live a life of trust and obedience, glorifying him by completing the specific work he gives me to do.

Bungee #4—Unconfessed Sin

As Christ-followers we have been justified by the life, work and sacrifice of Christ. Our righteousness before God has been established apart from anything we can do or have done. As Romans 8:1–2 says, "Therefore, there is now no condemnation for those who are in Christ Jesus, because through Christ Jesus the law of the Spirit who gives life has set you free from the law of sin and death." This is amazing news!

However, what God has done is not a license for sin. Paul knows that it might be easy for some people to be thinking this, so he writes, "What shall we say, then? Shall we go on sinning so that grace may increase? By no means! We are those who have died to sin; how can we live in it any longer?" (Romans 6:1–2).

In light of Christ's work and by the Holy Spirit's indwelling power, we are called to live holy lives. As 1 Peter 1:14–16 says, "As obedient children, do not conform to the evil desires you had when you lived in ignorance. But just as he who called you is holy, so be holy in all you do; for it is written: 'Be holy, because I am holy.'"

As we seek to live in holiness, everyone falls short. This doesn't impact our identity as God's children or the righteousness provided by Christ. Our sin does, however, negatively impact our relationship with God, with others and with ourselves. In response, we need to confess our sins and choose to repent.

Concealing our sins isn't an option. As Proverbs 28:13 says, "Whoever conceals their sins does not prosper, but the one who confesses and renounces them finds mercy." The application to bungees is that unconfessed sin in our lives is a bungee cord. Concealing our sins provides the right conditions for breeding them. Sin grows best in the dark. The by-products are equally bad. The by-products are guilt, shame, condemnation and defeat.

There are so many illustration options for this bungee. We are a creative people! However, one too common example of unconfessed sin for Christian leaders relates to the area of sexual purity. The use of pornography is at epidemic proportions and growing in the general population. Within the smaller segment of Christian leaders, the use of pornography is a common bungee cord that is often carefully concealed. This bungee can mire a passionate, gifted and competent leader in guilt, shame, condemnation and defeat. This inner turmoil then slowly undermines the passion, giftedness and competence.

In seeking to lead yourself well, it's critical to see unconfessed sin as a significant bungee cord and take action. Specifically, we are called to confess and repent. As 1 John 1:9 says, "If we confess our sins, he is faithful and ust and will forgive us our sins and purify us from all unrighteousness."

James 5:16 adds a community element and calls us to "confess your sins to each other and pray for each other so that you may be healed." This isn't required to receive forgiveness, but it does add another healthy and helpful dimension. The added humility required to confess a sin breaks the power of secrecy while also adding a healthy gravity. Bringing sin into a greater light with another person also helps to break its power, and the response of a brother or sister in Christ allows grace to be extended from another person on the journey.

For this bungee it is also important to look beyond surface. As just one example, the use of pornography can be often be a symptom of a much deeper unmet core need or unresolved issue. Unless we get beyond the symptom sin to the roots, we can get in a discouraging cycle where confession is followed quickly by relapse and even greater guilt. We will address this important topic in chapter 11— "Dealing with Dandelions."

Bungee #5—Believing Lies

We all remember the schoolyard adage "Sticks and stones will break my bones but names will never hurt me." Some of us chanted that refrain in hope of self-protection, yet many were still hurt by names in the schoolyard. Whether it was a name like "Stupid," "Fat," "Skinny," "Gay" or something much more creative, these names are lies. They are like modern day curses. Whether intentional or not, they can bring condemnation, shame, failure, oppression and even destruction.

As we shared this concept with an Arrow class, it hit close to home for one of our participants. He served as an executive pastor at a large church. They had been going through a season of downsizing, and in his role he had to tell several team members that they were being released from employment. After a number of these conversations, this servant leader was given the nickname "Axe Man" by his colleagues.

This nickname likely wasn't given with great malice in mind. However, for a Christian leader with a shepherd's heart, this nickname was an affront to his heart for God and love for the people. For a man who was making sacrifices to diligently serve the purposes of God, this nickname was completely counter to his very calling to shepherd and build up the body of Christ. Though he knew this label was not true, he began to wonder. And, as he shared this story, the tears that came illustrated the depth of hurt he had suffered.

His Arrow classmates responded. They called the nickname a lie. They encouraged him to reject this lie and curse in the authority of Jesus and to proclaim his identity in Christ. Then, they declared and prayed words of truth over him. These words of blessing reinforced his true identity. The bungee was broken.

Bungee #6—Lordship Issues

Jesus is both Savior and Lord. A core theme of the Christian life is that Christ-followers must live lives of surrender in following Jesus. We can do nothing apart from Christ. He sustains us. We live by his grace, and we need his power.

So, when we take ownership of an area of our life, we are intentionally excluding God from that area. We are telling God that we are in control and that we do not want or need his involvement. It's like putting up a tall fence with a big sign that says "Keep Out." This is an affront to God, whom we have declared as Lord of all of our life. It also sets us up for failure. We cannot possibly effectively manage any area of our life in our own strength.

Sometimes these fences are made innocently, with good intentions or even for our own self-protection. For example, when growing up we might experience a destructive or harmful effect from a parent. In response, we make a declaration or a vow that "I will never be like my dad" or "I will never drink like my mom." Although there may be a solid reason to not be like Dad or Mom, we don't have the right or the resolve to make that promise to ourselves or anyone else. It's actually prideful to do so. Besides, we are called to be like Jesus only, not like anyone else. This vow immediately becomes a burden that we cannot carry. We are trying to control part of our life apart from the grace and power of God.

To give another example, if someone is hurt deeply in a physical or emotional way, that person may vow to "never let myself be hurt like that again." Trying to fulfill this vow might mean putting up emotional walls to keep other people at a distance. The result, however, isn't the healing and wholeness that God desires to bring. The result is greater dysfunction and an exhausting battle to try to control an area of life.

One more example is a vow like "I will never finish second again." This can lead to a drivenness to win and prove yourself to others. As a Christ-follower your identity is not based on winning, and your calling should be about seeking "first his kingdom and his righteousness" (Matthew 6:33). In short, nothing good can come from a vow.

Addressing bungee cords related to lordship issues involves taking inventory. This means reflecting on key moments in your life. Did you make any vows or did you resolve to take control of an area of your life? I'm not referencing wedding vows that were made before God and with God's blessing and grace to fulfill them. The kind of vow I'm referring to is made apart from his lordship and by our own strength.

Sometimes nothing comes immediately to mind, so it's a good idea to pray and ask God to reveal any vows. You shouldn't try to manufacture something that's not there, but if you do discover a vow, confess it by name to God. In your prayer of confession you should also make a declarative statement that you entrust this area of your life to God and that he has lordship over it and all of you.

There are many other bungee cord possibilities. We should not be paranoid about bungees or the work of the evil one, but we are called to be alert. There is a spiritual battle underway, and you and I are targets. I believe that Christian leaders are high-value targets. If the evil one can distract, discourage, divide or destroy a Christian leader, there is significant collateral damage.

C. S. Lewis's classic *The Screwtape Letters* is a sobering book that imagines the schemes of the evil one as he targets individuals. The book stirred this question in me: If the evil one were to target an area of my life to seek my downfall, what area do I think he would target? This is a helpful reflection question. Are you aware of your weak spots and vulnerabilities? Is there anything in your life that is or could be a bungee cord?

Reflection Questions

1. Bungee cords can be related to spiritual, emotional, relational or competency issues in your life. Can you identify any bungee cords that may be holding you back right now?

2. As you read through the list of six common spiritual bungees (fear, unforgiveness, unconfessed sin, idolatry, lies, and lordship), did any of them resonate with you? If so, take action. Confess specifically and repent unequivocally.

3. If the evil one were seeking your downfall, what area do you think he would target? How can you guard this area? Pray and take any action steps.

Chapter 5

Key Practice #3

Keeping Connected

Every morning during their early months of training, the first paratroopers in the US Army's 506th Parachute Infantry Regiment would take a three-mile run up a steep long hill called "Currahee." Sometimes these young soldiers from Easy Company would make the run weighed down with full packs. Once at the top, they would then run back down. Day after day they would run three miles up and three miles down. Sometimes they would even choose to voluntarily repeat this grueling drill at night to ready themselves for the critical mission that lay ahead.

The name "Currahee" means "We stand alone together," and this hill became an icon for the deep comradery and lifelong community that these young men forged as they prepared for the D-Day invasion of Normandy and the battles beyond. Each paratrooper did "stand alone" at the airplane door before jumping out into the line of live enemy fire. However, they lived, fought, suffered and overcame seemingly overwhelming obstacles "together." As the award-winning HBO miniseries *Band of Brothers* shares, "They depended on each other, and the world depended on them"—a powerful statement of deep friendship, profound community and compelling purpose.

This story is a clear reminder that in many ways we do "stand alone" but we also "stand together." Dietrich Bonhoeffer explains this paradox in *Life Together*. He writes,

> Alone you stood before God when God called you. Alone you had to obey God's voice. Alone you had to take up your cross, struggle and pray and alone you will die and give account to God. You cannot avoid yourself, for it is precisely God who has singled you out. If you do not want to be alone, you are rejecting Christ's call to you, and you can have no part in the community of those who are called.[1]

However, while we do "stand alone," we do so "together." Focusing on this togetherness, Bonhoeffer goes on to remind readers of the communal aspect of the Christian faith:

> You are called into the community of faith; the call was not meant for you alone. You carry your cross, you struggle, and you pray in the community of faith, the community of those who are called. You are not alone even when you die, and on the day of judgment you will be only one member of the great community of faith of Jesus Christ.[2]

Bonhoeffer's words and the young soldiers running up Currahee are poignant reminders that we cannot fully experience the life God desires for us on our own. We have been created for relationship, and we desperately need to be part of community. Our growth in Christ is a corporate endeavor. It's not a private and individualistic one. To lead ourselves well we need the prayers, encouragement, example, teaching, challenge, resources, support, friendship, accountability, gifts and so much more that flow from relationships and community.

Unfortunately, despite living in an age when we have hundreds of Facebook "friends" and LinkedIn connections, too many Christ-followers and even Christian leaders are only virtually connected to relationships and community. So many of us struggle with loneliness and long for deep connections but cannot seem to cultivate true community in the frantic pace of our mobile 24/7/365 world.

Many others intentionally insulate themselves from community as a measure of self-protection. We hesitate to expose our real selves, fearing rejection, betrayal or being wounded. We sense that professional boundaries need to be maintained at the cost of deeper relationships. For many people it seems far safer to wear a mask and keep others at a distance or a surface level. In fact, many pastors have been encouraged to avoid deep friendships within their churches for fear of blurring the lines of accountability or trust. Ensuring our own constant state of busyness is one way to maintain a layer of supposed protection. One of the outcomes of all this is loneliness.

Mobility is another force that can work against relational connectivity. Few people live in the same community over a lifetime or even for very long. Whether we move for work or for other reasons, it is hard to maintain past relationships and can be difficult to cultivate new ones.

Seasons of trial and challenge can also undermine deep relationships. For starters, it can seem too painful to reach out. Inviting others into our private world can also offend our pride or potentially shatter our public persona.

There are also the "nobody" lies that can gain a foothold in our minds. These lies are subtle but powerful. It's easy to believe that nobody really cares, nobody can really understand or nobody can help.

Buying into this kind of mindset leads to isolation. The consequences are enormous. As the best-selling authors and Christian psychologists Henry Cloud and John Townsend comment, "Virtually every emotional and psychological problem, from addictions to depression, has alienation or emotional isolation at its core or close to it."[3]

Isolation also plays into the hand of the evil one. If you've ever watched National Geographic documentaries, you've seen lions zeroing in on the prey that get separated from their pack. Applying this concept to the spiritual realm, we need to remember that the evil one "prowls around like a roaring lion looking for someone to devour" (1 Peter 5:8). In other words, when you step outside the protection and provision of community, you are a much easier target and much more vulnerable.

Living in isolation is a common struggle for Christian leaders. It's ironic that leaders who are often in the midst of people are not personally engaged in deep relationships or community. The consequences can be stark. As Bill Hybels writes,

> I don't want to be a prophet of doom, but I am afraid that a steady stream of church leaders are going to disappear tragically from the rosters of kingdom leadership unless they commit themselves to discovering safe people and leaning into those relationships. Our hearts were not built to handle the hardships and heartaches of ministry alone.[4]

As Hybels encourages leaders to "lean *into*" safe people, I remember one Arrow leader who chose to lean *out* of community. After her first residential session she simply dropped off the relational radar. She didn't respond to emails from our office or calls from her peer group. Finally, she sent an email and explained that she had been going through a health issue and a very difficult season of life. She wrote that it was just too hard to share her situation with others.

I could understand her reluctance to share her struggle. I'm both an introvert and a fairly private person. I've been in difficult circumstances when everything inside me wanted to turn inward and lean away from relationships. Though I could understand this leader's mindset, my heart broke for her and what she missed. Had she chosen to lean into a safe community and shared her situation, she would have been deeply cared for and blessed. Rather than being isolated and on her own, she would have received prayer, encouragement, protection, practical help and support. Her vulnerability would have deepened her connection with her peers, and her example would have encouraged others to go deeper and be more vulnerable too.

Both Paul and Jesus beautifully modeled the importance of relationships and leaning into community. Paul's example reminds us that even in the midst of hardship, community is critical. The list of challenges he experienced as a servant of God is daunting. In 2 Corinthians 6:3–10, he makes a laundry list of hardships. He cites distresses, beatings, imprisonments, riots, hard work, sleepless nights, hunger, dishonor, being regarded as an imposter, sorrow and having nothing as some of the challenges he faced. Yet these things did not turn him inward or isolate him from community.

Instead, Paul actually challenges the Corinthians to respond with more openness. In verse 11–13, Paul says, "We have spoken freely to you, Corinthians, and opened wide our hearts to you. We are not withholding our affection from you, but you are withholding yours from us. As a fair exchange…open wide your hearts also." If anybody had a solid case for "taking my ball and going home," it was Paul. He had been through more than enough. Yet he didn't withhold his affection from the Corinthians. He leaned in. He challenged them to do the same.

Jesus' life was also one of deep relationships and leaning into community. He lived, loved, served and suffered in the context of community. He spent the majority of his time with his small group of disciples. He invested deeply in the 3, the 12, and the 72. He invited people not to simply learn from him or be led by him but to be *with* him.

Jesus' last moments of freedom at Gethsemane provide a powerful illustration of leaning in. These were his final minutes before he would be betrayed, arrested and deserted and die a terrible death. These moments were his crucible moments. Yet, in these final moments, he chose to bring along his inner circle.

It's true that Peter, James and John didn't fully understand Jesus' situation. In Jesus' crucible moment, they drifted off to sleep three times. Clearly, they weren't going to win any awards for being present, supportive or compassionate. But, despite the imperfection of his community, Jesus chose to lean into community and relationships rather than isolate himself. As James Lawrence writes,

> [Jesus] shared his whole life with them, not just his public ministry. He was committed to investing in others and sharing his Father's vision for his life, even though they struggled to accept it (Mark 8:31–33). I find this challenging because it speaks of vulnerability (seen clearly when the disciples let him down in his hour of need), interdependence (as the disciples provide for his needs), and recognition that others were needed to fulfill the next stage of what he came to do.[5]

To follow Christ's example and to lead ourselves well, we need healthy relationships. We need to choose to lean into community, even when it's not perfect.

We need to be and to keep connected.

In *Connecting*,[6] Robert Clinton and Paul Stanley provide a helpful model for intentionally seeking out and cultivating a constellation model of mentoring. The uniqueness of their approach is that, rather than viewing mentoring as a distinct and isolated one-to-one relationship, they advocate a model where each leader develops a 360-degree community of support. Rather than seeking out just one mentor, they encourage a rich and diverse constellation of support that includes multiple connection points.

If we apply this model beyond mentoring to our overall relational connections, we can identify our need for multiple kinds and layers of relationships and community. Without this kind of constellation, we become isolated. With a constellation we invite others to support, shape and sharpen us. To provide some examples to get you thinking about developing your relational constellation, here are a few snapshots from my own constellation model:

Family—Just before I left home for university, I became a Christ-follower. As I tried to figure out my new faith, I naively decided to write a letter. I was sensing a call to ministry, and I wanted to learn more about apologetics, speaking and youth ministry. So I wrote to Josh McDowell. Josh was and is a well-known Christian author and speaker. He has written many books, and a couple of them helped me come to faith. In my letter I asked if I could travel with him and learn along the way.

To my surprise, I received a response inviting me to apply for a year-long internship program. I applied and was accepted. I had the privilege of travelling all over the world and learning many wonderful lessons. But the most important lesson I learned was one I never expected. The biggest lesson was watching Josh love his wife and spend time with his four children. From a front-row seat, I watched him live out his own words: "I never let my family come before my ministry. My family is my first ministry."

At times Josh went to great length to keep his family as his first ministry. Sometimes this meant driving all night after a speaking engagement so he could be home for breakfast when his family woke up. I watched Josh, with a travel schedule that was packed and exhausting for his three twenty-something interns, attend twenty or more of his son Sean's twenty-three senior high basketball games. Sometimes this required flying the red-eye. Sometimes this meant saying no to great opportunities. Whatever it took, Josh walked the talk.

The takeaway for me is a reminder that my wife, Lea, and three kids are great and precious gifts. I have been told "Enjoy them now; they will grow up fast" by enough older parents that I believe it. And I know that when I move on from my work role, only these four will join me in the moving truck. For their benefit and my own, they need to be primary connections in my life.

For me, being intentionally connected with family means prioritizing regular date nights and semi-annual nights away with Lea. It means ensuring that family vacations are scheduled and taken every year. It means leaving my iPhone at the front door when I get home from work so I can be fully present. It means eating meals together whenever possible. It means taking a weekly Sabbath together and trying to find special time with each child before a long road trip. It means digging deep for extra energy to go outside to play with the kids after a long day—for my benefit and theirs.

Friendships—After moving to the west coast and starting a busy role with lots of travel, I didn't see much room for friendships. Keeping connected with family and one step ahead at work seemed to fill my plate. Yet, I still longed for friendships. I sensed a similar longing in some friends from church, so I proposed a monthly small group gathering called "Band of Brothers." It's now short-formed "BOB," but it has been a place of rich and deep connection. The format is fairly simple. We meet once a month to watch and discuss an episode of HBO's *Band of Brothers*, enjoy some great snacks, catch up and pray for one another.

Connecting monthly with these brothers has laid the relational foundation to send out a text message requesting prayer or practical help during the week. For all of us, it has made a difference to know that we are not alone. We know that there are three other guys who know us and are there if and when we need them.

Church—Dr. Eddie Gibbs served for many years as a professor at Fuller Seminary. The Church has been his focus of study, writing and teaching for many decades. During an Arrow residential session, he made a brief comment that I hope I never forget. In talking about the Church, he said, "She's not optional."

Those three words are prophetic for our day. In our overextended lives, it is tempting to put our connection to a local church body in the optional category. Add in our propensity to lean out of community for any number of reasons, and it's little wonder that attending church twice per month is seen as regular attendance and committed participation.

For too many, church is seen not as a "get to" but as an "ought to" or "have to." It's important to remember that we are designed to function as a body. We get to gather together as a church body every week. We get to see and hear brothers and sisters in the midst of deep struggles sing praise to God. We get to pray for and encourage one another. We get to sing God's praises and hear God's Word. We get to remember that we are not alone. We get to serve and contribute our gifts to projects we could never do on our own. We get to be part of a local and global community of Christ-followers.

Being Mentored—Everyone needs one or more mentors to provide the depth of reflection necessary to sustain vision and energy for life and leadership. I also believe that everyone who can should serve as a mentor—because the mentor learns as much from the process as the one being mentored.

I have been deeply blessed through a number of formal and informal mentoring relationships over the years. In the formal mentoring relationships, I have sought out mature Christians whom I respect. I look for safe, real and wise people who listen deeply, ask great questions, are encouragers and provide fresh perspective. I ask them to meet monthly or quarterly for a defined season to invite their input, wisdom, experience, counsel and encouragement in specific areas in my life.

Formal mentors are a great gift and need to be treated like gold. This means that you do your best to make it easy for them to mentor you. For example, I would suggest that you initiate the meetings (never leave a mentoring meeting without the next date set), send a brief update and agenda ahead of connecting, drive to them, pay for the meal or coffee, reschedule only in case of extreme emergency and redirect the conversation to what is most helpful for you.

I have also found it very helpful to define the season for mentoring before you get started. Not setting an end to your formal mentoring relationship can lead to relational fatigue, frustration and awkwardness. One of you may be ready to stop the relationship, but trying to do so might be taken the wrong way.

To help avoid this challenge, you can agree up front on a timeframe. For example, you could agree to meet for a school or ministry year. When this time period is over, you review and celebrate progress together. Then, thank your mentor and share with him or her the impact made in your life. After spending this time together, it will also be quite natural for you both to agree to reconnect on occasion in the future.

In informal mentoring relationships, you may not use the formal term "mentor," but mentoring is what happens. In terms of format, it may be an occasional phone call or breakfast meeting to ask the informal mentor to be a sounding board or to offer specific expertise about a particular issue. My informal mentors have been a treasure chest of wisdom and support.

I recently read a beautiful letter from a mentee about a mentor. The mentor was Gib Martin. Gib was a pastor for over forty years at the same church in the Seattle area. He loved God deeply, loved the Church passionately and dearly loved mentoring younger leaders. On the day Gib died, one of his mentees from the Arrow Leadership Program wrote these words:

> Along with my Bible, two books are speaking God's truth into my life today. Both were recommended by Gib, a man whose life intersected mine only seven years ago through the Arrow Leadership Program. Gib's fatherly wisdom, his authenticity, his love, his acceptance, and his grace have profoundly influenced my life.
>
> Into my brokenness Gib spoke God's truth. These books call me into authentic relationships with God and others. They nudge me out of hiding, toward the blessing of being known, accepted and loved. These thoughts have been the message of Gib's life to mine. The books simply affirm the message he's shared with me in our conversations and lived out in our relationship.
>
> Though we had a face-to-face relationship for only a mere three weeks of our lives, we spoke by phone on an occasional basis for the past 7 years. Gib knew me and I knew him.
>
> He taught me that friendship goes both ways—I have to be willing to express myself and to initiate and that sometimes this means taking risks. I can only pray that the gift God gave me through watching Gib's life and through my relationship with him spills over into the lives of many others as I bravely accept the call to transparency, friendship, and right living.

This letter is a powerful reminder of the profound impact a mentor can have in your life. It's also a beautiful billboard encouraging us to actively engage as mentors.

Being a Mentor—Mentoring others is a profound privilege and a strategic opportunity to influence others. After I started as an intern alongside Josh McDowell I asked him why he had decided to develop an internship program to mentor younger men. He responded that when he was my age he had written to the Christian leaders of the day asking for mentoring. He was repeatedly turned down. So he decided that if he ever had the opportunity to intentionally invest in others he would do and share whatever he could.

Now, several decades later, dozens of young men have had their lives changed through Josh's intentional investment. This cadre of interns is now scattered across the world, impacting others.

Many people are overwhelmed or intimidated by the term "mentor." They feel underqualified or fearful of messing up someone else in some way. If this is your perspective, it's encouraging to remember that ultimately Jesus is the primary mentor. You are directing people to follow him and to allow him to do his work.

We recently surveyed the on-site mentors for the Arrow Leadership Program. One of the questions was "How fulfilled are you through your role?" Their response was nearly unanimous—highly fulfilled. They gave this response because they are blessed by the opportunity to invest in others. They learn from their mentees. They are stirred to depend on God more as they try to walk alongside someone else. They grow to care deeply for their mentee and appreciate their mentee's care for them.

Spiritual Direction—A spiritual director is a trained Christian professional who helps clients to cultivate their spiritual life through prayerful reflection, listening to God, spiritual exercises and conversation. Although spiritual direction has been more common in the Roman Catholic tradition, there is a growing spiritual direction movement in Protestant circles today.

My initial introduction to spiritual direction came through a weekend silent retreat. The idea of thirty-six hours of absolute silence seemed daunting at first, but as a contemplative and introvert I was also drawn to the experience. Plus there was one built-in outlet each day for conversation. Each participant was scheduled to have one hour with a spiritual director.

During my daily spiritual direction appointment, my director started by lighting a candle to symbolize the presence of Christ and inviting me to a time of silent prayer. Then the director began to ask deep questions. These questions encouraged me to reflect on God's work in, through and around me.

I've met with a spiritual director monthly for one hour for the last couple of years. Most of the time, I bring an issue or two to discuss. It has been a safe and rich rhythm that forces me to slow down, to explore what is going on in my soul and to reflect on what God is seeking to say and do in my life.

Coach—Record-setting professional athletes choose to have coaches to help them get to the next level, and it follows that all of us can reap benefits from engaging coaches to help us personally and professionally. A trained coach can help facilitate a highly intentional process of self-discovery, skill development and problem solving.

Through monthly one-hour meetings, my coach helped me to identify and work through a number of personal and professional growth areas. Using her extensive experience in a variety of settings, she asked penetrating questions that forced me to get to the roots of issues. The monthly rhythm of accountability to take practical next steps was another great benefit from coaching.

Peers—Ten years ago I moved over 3,000 miles to join the team at Arrow Leadership. In this new role and being so far from home, I knew I desperately needed a support network of peers. However, I also knew that it would take time in my new setting to meet the right people. So I contacted two longtime friends in Ontario and asked if we could meet virtually by Skype for three hours every quarter.

This format gives each of us one hour, in which we provide a brief update on life and share one current challenge and then the two others coach, consult, challenge, pray and encourage. When the hour is up, we go on to the next peer and his hour.

I love this group because we can share anything and everything about life in the context of safety. We trust one another deeply—and after ten years together we have enough history on one another that we have to trust one another. From this foundation of safety we move toward practical help, support and transformation in each of our lives. We can relate to similar stage of life issues, we know each other well enough that we can read between the lines when each of us share, and we expect each other to speak truthfully. The practical input is also a great gift that leverages our different personalities, gifts and experiences.

Normal People—I first heard this term during my first residential session of the Arrow Leadership Program. At first I wondered, "What do they mean by 'normal people'?" I soon discovered that this was a term to describe people who don't yet follow Jesus. Instead of the term "non-Christian," which seems to be exclusive insider-and-outsider language, the term "normal people" is a reminder that in our culture it's usually normal to **not** follow Jesus. Christ-followers are the outsiders. We are the "aliens and strangers" (1 Peter 2:11, NASB) in this world.

That first Arrow residential session challenged me to more intentionally care about and lovingly engage normal people in my sphere of influence. This means embracing my role as an ambassador for Christ and seeking to lead more to Jesus. In practical terms, this doesn't need to be complicated. It starts with prayer and involves regularly praying for normal people.

Pastor and Arrow trainer Dr. Dave Overholt encourages the simple step of being 10 percent more friendly. Just taking an extra interest in people, asking questions, really listening and practically serving others can open up opportunities for much deeper conversations.

Finding your third space is another practical step. If home and work are your primary places of presence, where is your third space? Maybe you belong to a club, volunteer for a community service or play a sport. This third space is a natural place for you to be, so it can also become a natural place for you to connect with normal people.

Finally, we are called to be ready. As 1 Peter 3:15 says, "Always be prepared to give an answer to everyone who asks you to give the reason for the hope that you have. But do this with gentleness and respect." When the opportunity arises, you need to be ready to share the good news of Christ.

Connecting with normal people isn't just about sharing your faith with others. It's also about the effect sharing your faith has on you. It stirs you to pray, to trust, to be an example, to depend, and to learn.

These ideas are just a sampling of intentional ways to be and keep relationally connected. Keeping connected helps you to lead yourself more effectively. To borrow from HBO's *Band of Brothers*, as Christ-followers and Christian leaders may we depend on Christ and one another, knowing that the world is depending on us.

Reflection Questions

1. Is your natural default to lean into community or away from it? Why?

2. Who would you bring with you to a "Gethsemane" moment of great trial? Why?

3. Draw a "constellation model of relationships" in your life. Get a blank piece of paper. Put "Me" in the middle and draw lines to label people groups to whom you are connected. Then reflect on these questions:

   a. Are you deeply connected in multiple ways? Is there anything missing?

   b. How could you be more intentional with each people group?

   c. Who should you be spending more time with?

   d. Are those in your key relationships getting time with you at your best?

Chapter 6

Key Practice #4

Taking Care of Me, Part 1

"Wow! Everybody's FAT!"[1]
This blunt observation opens Rick Warren's book *The Daniel Plan: 40 Days to a Healthier Life*. As founding pastor of Saddleback Church in southern California, Rick had just spent the day baptizing over 800 adults. Clearly, it was a memorable day. After all, can you imagine a baptism service that large?

Beyond the spiritual celebration, it was also memorable for Rick because he literally felt the growing epidemic of obesity as he lowered people under the water, then lifted them back up. He was also personally convicted. He recognized that he was as out of shape as everyone else. But, even more convicting, he realized that he was setting a terrible example with his own health.

This baptism service was an unexpected wake-up call for Rick Warren. It led to significant changes in his life, and it led to the development of a program called The Daniel Plan. Rick's wake-up call is needed across North America.

A wake-up call is needed because we are in the midst of an epidemic. Despite the billions of dollars spent annually on gym memberships, exercise contraptions, diet fads and wellness programs, the statistics on poor physical health are simply staggering. Here are just a few statistics on the obesity epidemic:

- More than 35% of American adults are obese; another third are overweight.[2] That's two-thirds of the population, and the figures are growing.[3]

- 31% of Canadian children are overweight or obese.[4]

- More people are suffering from the result of too much food than from malnutrition.[5]

87

- The New England Journal of Medicine in a study of over 1,000,000 adults during a fourteen-year period found that being overweight shortened a person's life.[6]

- In the USA, obesity counts for approximately 18% of deaths.[7]

- $147 billion (in 2008 dollars) is spent annually in medical costs, and obesity/physical inactivity is close to overtaking smoking as the most preventable cause of death.[8]

Surprisingly, the Church in North America, except for a few efforts like the Daniel Plan, is conspicuously silent on this issue. We know that millions of people, both inside and outside the Church, are struggling with their weight. In fact, a recent study from Duke Divinity School found that this problem affects clergy at a greater level. The study of UMC clergy in North Carolina found 41 percent obese, which is 10 percent higher than the state's general population.[9]

We know that billions of dollars are spent in related medical bills, costs to lost productivity or trying to change and become healthier. In fact, of the almost $3 trillion dollars in spent every year in the American health care system, almost 80 percent is for chronic lifestyle preventable and reversible disease.[10]

The obesity epidemic is just one component of the much broader matter of physical health. Sleep, nutrition, exercise, rest and renewal are all key elements. Unfortunately, the statistics are equally discouraging for these key factors too.

The bottom line is that our physical health matters to God. Our body is a gift entrusted to our care and stewardship. It's also incredibly important for leading ourselves. Our physical health and energy provide the fuel that is a prime determinant of our capacity and output as well as our overall wellness.

Research demonstrates that there is a clear correlation between our physical health and our emotional, mental and spiritual vigor. As Jim Loehr writes in *The Power of Story*,

> With more physical energy, you can engage more deeply on a physical level—that's obvious—but you can do so on a greater emotional, mental and spiritual level, too. If you do not maximize your physical energy through proper nutrition, exercise and rest, then you simply cannot maximize the other three types of energy.[11]

As an example, when I am physically depleted, I often see the impact on my emotions. My thinking gets cloudy, my resolve diminishes, I become more sensitive to criticism, my fuse toward anger is shorter and my susceptibility to fear and negative thinking increases. As the football legend Vince Lombardi said, "Fatigue makes cowards of us all."

Furthermore, if I'm physically depleted, not only are my emotions more fragile but my mental capacity is also negatively affected. When I lack energy, I'm less alert. I have more trouble with concentration, and I am less creative. This mental fog also impacts what Loehr calls our spiritual energy. This is defined as our ability to connect deeply with our purpose and to make a significant contribution as a difference maker.

A by-product of this pattern is that we can quickly find ourselves spiraling into an energy deficit. As Loehr explains, "Without proper exercise, nutrition, and rest, the body slowly begins to break. You're operating at a perpetual deficit. You're always exhausted. You're seriously disengaged. Your body is now in survival mode."[12] At this point it becomes harder and harder to break the cycle and return to health.

As Christ-followers, our bodies are temples of the Holy Spirit. As 1 Corinthians 6:19–20 rhetorically asks, "Do you not know that your bodies are temples of the Holy Spirit, who is in you, whom you have received from God? You are not your own; you were bought at a price. Therefore honor God with your bodies." This verse needs to be first read in the context of sexual purity, but we can safely assume that honoring God with our body in every way is central to following Jesus.

Healthy stewardship of our physical health is even more important for Christian leaders. Leaders are examples and need to take the lead to personally model good physical stewardship. If those we serve see us taking care of ourselves, they will be more encouraged to take care of themselves.

Leaders also need to keep focused on the mission. However, you can only maximize your focus on the mission long-term if you take good care of yourself. If you don't have energy or you are dealing with health concerns, your focus will move off mission and on to your physical health.

At this point, it's important to point out an added challenge for Christian leaders. This challenge is self-care. Self-care often takes a back seat for Christian leaders. When Christian leaders see enormous needs around them, there is a deep desire to meet those needs—even at a sacrificial personal cost. However, as flight attendants say during the safety demonstration segment about the oxygen mask, "Please make sure to secure your own mask before assisting others." On a plane, if you don't secure your own mask first, you may be overcome by the cabin decompression and become unable to function or help anyone else. In other words, it's actually best for you and others if you first ensure that your own mask is working. Similarly, if you don't first take care of yourself physically, you may become unable to function or unable to help others.

In seeking to steward physical health, we need to guard against embracing the prominent cultural pressure to idolize the body and embrace vanity. We also need to recognize that many of us have some physical limitations or challenges. These aren't permission to ignore our physical side, but rather are a call to steward the resources we have as best we can.

Being on the cover of a fitness magazine isn't the goal. Gary Thomas writes in *Every Body Matters* that we are not called to be *ornaments*. Instead we are to be *instruments* set apart for God. If the instrument isn't ready or able, it can't do the good work God desires. In plain terms, if we are physically incapacitated because of our own lack of self-care, we are not able to do what God has called us to do.

Thomas reframes the right reason for keeping in shape. It isn't to turn heads on the beach. As he writes,

> The reason I want to get in shape then, the reason I long for God's church to get in shape, is not to impress anyone, not to make others feel inferior, not to demonstrate my own personal discipline and self-control. God forbid! On the contrary, it is to become, as Paul writes, "instruments for special purposes, made holy, useful to the Master and prepared to do any good work."[13]

Ironically, our traditional focus on stewarding our souls and viewing our bodies as almost necessary evils is more than unbiblical. Lack of physical stewardship actually undercuts the stewarding of our souls. If we lose physical self-control and discipline, that effects our soul. If food becomes an idol, that effects our soul. If our energy is depleted or we are sick, that can effect our soul.

Let's flip this argument around to the positive. Imagine stewarding your physical health so well that you not only have more energy in your day but you extend your lifespan by years. This means that as an instrument for special purposes, you can do years more of good works. It also means that you can be around for your family and friends a lot longer.

National Geographic's Blue Zone[14] research project illustrates how physical stewardship can radically change health trends and extend lifespans. In this project, researchers scoured the planet to explore where and why some people groups live longer than others. Surprisingly, one of these groups was located in Loma Linda in southern California.

This group of Seventh Day Adventists takes physical health seriously. They have adopted a lifestyle that incorporates healthy diet, exercise, play and rest. As a result they have the longest life expectancy in the nation.[15] One study found that on average a 30-year-old Adventist male will live 7.3 years longer than an average 30-year-old Californian male. A 30-year-old Adventist female gains 4.4 years of life over a Californian woman of the same age.[16] If you filter the study and look at 30-year-old Seventh Day vegetarians, the average man's extra life expectancy jumps to 9.5 years and the average woman's 6.1 years.[17]

There is some good news. For starters, raising the bar on your physical health doesn't need to be complicated or costly. You don't need to go on a kale-only diet. There are some very simple and accessible best practices that can begin to make an immediate difference.

Another note of good news is that taking action on these simple and accessible best practices can make a positive impact. In fact, we can even begin to see reversal of the damage that has been done. A study by Dr. Dean Ornish supports this conclusion and shows that "lifestyle changes that include diet and exercise can reverse the atherosclerotic change of coronary heart disease and unblock arteries enough to avoid surgery."[18]

The case for the critical need to steward your physical health is clear. It's time to move on to practical next steps. Chapter 7 will outline best practices that can make a significant difference related to the four key areas of sleep, nutrition, exercise and rest and renewal.

Reflection Questions

1. Why do you think physical stewardship has been such a challenge for so many?

2. What has been your approach to physical stewardship?

3. How does the concept of being "an instrument" for God's special purposes affect your thinking and theology about physical stewardship?

4. What differences do you think it could make for you—physically, emotionally, mentally and spiritually—to take your physical health to another level?

Chapter 7

Key Practice #4

Taking Care of Me, Part 2

L
eading yourself well includes taking care of yourself. In fact, taking care of yourself physically is a leverage point for managing your emotions, increasing your energy, focusing your mind, maximizing your influence and even extending your life. Physical stewardship is a spiritual discipline to help you live out your calling to be "instruments for special purposes, made holy, useful to the Master and prepared to do any good work" (2 Timothy 2:21).

This chapter focuses on providing practical action steps for each of the four key physical stewardship areas of sleep, nutrition, exercise and rest and renewal. Read on with the goal of identifying practical next steps to take your physical stewardship to the next level.

Key #1—Sleep

Sleep is critical. It's not a waste of time. It's also not a luxury. In fact, Tony Schwartz is one of many experts who argues that "No single behavior...more fundamentally influences our effectiveness in waking life than sleep."[1] This argument is backed up by overwhelming research that shows that great performers sleep more than the average person.

Unfortunately, people today are sleeping just 6.5 hours per day, which is nearly 2 hours less per day than 40 years ago.[2] It's also under the recommended sleep time of more than seven hours. In addition, more people are having challenges—from sleep apnea to insomnia—when they do try to sleep.

Not sleeping well or long enough creates a sleep deficit that the US Centers for Disease Control and Prevention calls a public health epidemic.[3] This deficit can lead to all kinds of problems. For starters, it can reduce efficiency, productivity and performance as well as lead to burnout. A study published in 2010 concluded that fatigue-related productivity loses were estimated to cost $1,967 per employee annually.[4]

Lack of sleep has numerous other consequences. It can also impair judgment and diminish concentration, negatively impact metabolism, reduce creativity, impair memory and motor skills, cloud thinking, trigger moodiness, increase stress and anxiety, and increase susceptibility of the immune system to illness and significant disease—including cardiovascular disease and some cancers.

If that list isn't enough, a sleep deficit also increases the risk of depression and suicidal thoughts, increases pain sensitivity and inflammation, and weakens your ability to judge subtle clues. Interestingly, lack of sleep can also impact eating and obesity. This works on two fronts. When you lack sleep, the hormone that makes you feel full decreases, and the hormone that tells your body to eat increases. As a result, you want to eat more than you would if you had slept more.

Author Greg McKeown argues in *Essentialism* that we are the best assets we have. In others words, if we want to maximize and make our highest contribution, McKeown argues, we need to take great care of ourselves. Unfortunately, he notes that "one of the most common ways people—especially ambitious, successful people—damage this asset is through lack of sleep."[5] This is actually backward. Sleep is not a waste of time to be eliminated. It's actually the foundation for great performance.

In fact, just as there are significant consequences of lack of sleep, there is a very positive impact when sleep is a priority. Contrary to what we see when someone goes to sleep, the body does not shut down. In reality, our brains are processing and our bodies healing as well as restoring. In one example, Stanford researcher Cheri D. Mah found that successful free-throw and three-point shooting increased by an average of 9 percent in practice for male basketball players who slept ten hours per night.[6]

Naps also provide rest and renewal. These brief sleeps have been found to provide positive results. For instance, NASA's Fatigue Counter Measures Program has found that a short nap of just forty minutes "improved performance by an average of 34 percent and alertness by one-hundred percent."[7] Similarly, night shift air traffic controllers who slept an average of nineteen minutes during a forty-minute nap break performed much better on tests that measured vigilance and reaction time.[8]

Though once cause for dismissal by most employers, naps have been embraced by Google. Their famous on-site nap pods have received great media attention in recent years. Employees can book nap times on request to refresh and re-energize themselves during the workday.

This practice goes back to one of history's great nappers, Winston Churchill. Churchill's naps were part of his daily regimen, especially during World War Two. Churchill said,

> You must sleep some time between lunch and dinner and no halfway measures...Don't think you will be doing less work because you sleep during the day. That's a foolish notion held by people who have no imagination. You will accomplish more. You get two days in one—well, at least one and a half, I'm sure. When the war started, I had to sleep during the day because that was the only way I could cope with my responsibilities."9

Last but not least, there is an important spiritual discipline behind sleep. When we choose to sleep we are acknowledging that we are not omnipotent like God. We need rest. We cannot do it all. Furthermore, by choosing to sleep we are choosing to trust God. As the psalmist writes, "In peace I will lie down and sleep, for you alone, LORD, make me dwell in safety" (Psalm 4:8).

Sleeping Well Tips

- Sleep in a quiet and dark space combined with a cooler temperature.

- Keep a regular bedtime and wake time (earlier for both is better).

- Develop a ritual leading up to bedtime that helps you relax. The discipline of a daily examen is one time-tested ritual designed to help you reflect and process your day with God. Also, you should avoid digital technology in the hours right before sleep.

- Keep your bed and bedroom clear of work-related papers and projects.

- Keep a notebook and pen at your bedside so you can write down and be free of "to do" items that come to mind as you try to get to sleep.

- Don't drink caffeine after mid-afternoon, and avoid alcohol after 8 p.m.

Key #2—Nutrition

These statistics may make you lose your appetite. Every year the average American consumes 29 pounds of french fries, 23 pounds of pizza, 24 pounds of ice cream, 53 gallons of soda, 24 pounds of artificial sweeteners, 2.7 pounds of salt and 90,000 milligrams of caffeine.[10]

You don't need a PhD in nutrition to know that this type of diet can't be good. Actually, that's a huge understatement. This kind of diet is catastrophic for weight control and disease prevention. The statistics are endless, so let's just talk about cancer.

Cancer is the second leading cause of death in America. An estimated 35 percent of cancers are related to diet. In fact, "there is a growing body of evidence that links poor food choices with higher incidence of cancer, particularly cancers of the esophagus, breast, prostate and colon."[11]

There is also a spiritual dimension to our use of food. In 1 Corinthians 10:31 Paul commands us, "So whether you eat or drink or whatever you do, do it all for the glory of God." Eating is a gift from God that we should enjoy. It is also a chance to slow down, change mental gears, be restored, seek refreshment, give thanks and enjoy the people around us.

Too many meals are gobbled down during commutes or in front of the television. Instead, consider stepping away from what you are doing and focusing on this time. Light a candle. Take a moment of reflective silence. Say a prayer of thanksgiving for God's provision and presence. Eat slowly and enjoy.

Food can also become an idol that can seriously impact other areas of our lives. Gary Thomas writes, "I go to war against gluttony because those who have walked closely with God warn me that overeating dulls me to God's accepting presence, makes me more vulnerable to other sins, negatively effects my relationships with other people and robs me of the joy rightfully mine as an adopted, deeply love and accepted child of God."[12]

A lack of knowledge about nutrition and a lack of financial resources to purchase healthy foods are two very practical issues behind the poor diet in North America. However, there are many simple and low-cost steps that can be taken to improve our diet and nutrition.

Eating Well Tips

- Water. Drink lots of it.

- Coffee drinkers, begin drinking at least one glass of water for every cup of coffee.

- Eat breakfast every day.

- Stop drinking soda and even diet drinks. One can of soda per day increases a kid's risk of obesity by 60 percent and a woman's chance of getting diabetes by more than 80 percent.[13]

- Cut out white sugar wherever possible. Be aware of all the alternate names for sugar and especially high fructose corn syrup (HFCS).

- If you take more calories in than you burn off, you will gain weight. For example, a middle-age man working a sedentary job who has a daily exercise program needs about 2,000 calories per day to maintain his weight. If he decides to stop at McDonald's today and order a Big Mac combo (with large fries and a medium Coke), he will consume 1,310 calories and 56 grams of fat (86 percent of his daily amount).[14] This means that eating much more during the rest of the entire day will add more calories than are burned off. Over time, this will lead to weight gain.

- Not all fats are equal. Some types of fats, such as the monounsaturated fats in nuts and olive oil and the omega-3 fatty acids found in fish and flaxseeds, help to boost mood and energy, as well as quell hunger.[15] Fats found in nuts, nut butters, olives and olive oil, avocados, soybeans and some types of fish help support your heart, fight cancer, reduce muscle damage from exercise and more.

- Don't eat after 8 p.m., because you won't likely be moving enough to burn off any of the calories.

- Despite all the conflicting nutritional research, overwhelming evidence suggests that a healthy dietary ratio is 50% to 60% complex carbohydrates, 25% to 35% protein, and 20% to 25% fat.[16]

- Look for simple ways to reduce fat. For example, you can remove the skin from chicken or turkey, go cheeseless, move from 2% milk to 1%, then to skim, and ask for sauces and dressings to be put on the side at restaurants.

- Take time to read labels and nutrition guides before you buy the product. What looks like a healthy choice may not actually be a healthy choice. It makes sense that a salad would be the healthiest option, but the creamy dressing may put it in the same fat bracket as a hamburger.

- Enjoy a small portion (one handful, not handfuls) of healthy snacks every couple of hours. This will help maintain your energy level, minimize cravings and reduce overcompensating and overeating at mealtimes.

- Stock your workplace cupboards with healthy snacks to help avoid unhealthy spur-of-the-moment purchases. Nuts are a healthy alternative.

- Eat slowly. This not only allows you to enjoy your food more but provides time for your body to tell you that you are satisfied. Stop eating when you are satisfied rather than full.

- Reduce high-sugar snacks and drinks. Replace with low-glycemic snacks. These include fruits like apples, cherries, grapefruits, oranges, peaches, plums and tomatoes. Food like eggs, green vegetables, meats, nuts, peanut butter, chickpeas, and yogurt are also on the list. Keep away from high-glycemic foods like bagels, cakes, candy, crackers, doughnuts, pretzels, and potato-based foods.

Key #3—Exercise

Exercise is another key to stewarding our physical health. Again, the statistics around lack of exercise are of great concern, and the benefits of exercise are clear. Here are just a few statistics:

- Only 15% of Americans regularly engage in vigorous physical activity for twenty minutes a day at least three times a week, despite the fact that the *Journal of the American Medical Association* notes that "regular exercise acts like a vaccine on the immune system."[17] Regular exercise also improves mental health and well-being and enhances mental functioning while reducing depression and anxiety.

- A study at the Cooper Institute for Aerobics Research of more than 10,000 men and 3,000 women found that men and women with low levels of physical fitness had more than twice the mortality rate of those with even a moderate level of physical fitness.[18] Fitness helped reduced risk for all causes of death, including diabetes, cancer and heart disease.

- The Harvard Medical School psychiatry professor John Ratey, author of *Spark: The Revolutionary New Science of Exercise and the Brain*, has found that regular physical activity not only improves brain function but also helps to combat depression and anxiety.[19]

Just as with sleep and nutrition, the positive benefits of exercise are clear. There are also many simple low-cost steps that you can incorporate into your daily routine to begin to see positive results. Here are a few:

Exercise Well Tips

• Try to get moving every 90 minutes during the workday. You can do this with simple practices like taking the stairs, going for a walking meeting, parking in a spot that makes you walk across the parking lot, scheduling midday exercise, pausing meetings for stretch breaks or walking around an airport terminal instead of sitting at the gate waiting to sit on the plane.

• Do some form of physical activity for at least twenty minutes daily.

• Mix strength and cardiovascular exercises.

• Change the intensity level of your exercise and have some intervals of more-intense exercise paired with intervals of less-intense exercise.

One additional related best practice is to get to the doctor. If you have access to health care, use it proactively with the goal of prevention. Taking time for yearly physicals, dental appointments and eye exams isn't a waste of time. Rather, it's good stewardship.

Key #4—Rest and Renewal

Remember Aesop's fable about the tortoise and the hare? The traditional moral of the story is that the tortoise's approach—slow, steady and persevering—is the right one. However, this "just-keep-going-never-stop-to-rest" approach doesn't hold up well under biblical or empirical scrutiny.

From a biblical perspective, God intentionally punctuates life with different rhythms. He created the rhythms of night and day. He designed the body to function on a rhythm of waking and sleeping. He made different seasons of the year. He established the rhythm of rest, renewal and worship through the Sabbath. He instituted the rhythm of feasts, festivals and ordinances for His people to gather, pause, celebrate and worship.

Empirical evidence also indicates that people function best in a rhythm of activity balanced by rest and renewal. Unfortunately, North Americans are buying into the tortoise approach minus the slow part. Most are trying to live a non-stop, 24/7/365, ever-connected, "always on" lifestyle. One example of this reality is found in our aversion to taking vacation time. Here are some puzzling statistics:

- The average American left 9.2 vacation days unused in 2012—up from 6.2 days in 2011.[20]

- Nearly one in five (18 percent) of Canadians say they won't take all the vacation days they are entitled to in 2014, and 13 percent say they'll take less time off this year than last (up from 9 percent in 2013).[21]

The consequences of not taking vacations are sobering. In addition to missed opportunities to create lifelong memories with family and friends, there are physical costs. These include a significantly greater chance of heart attack and premature death. On the psychological side, those who took vacations twice a year were half as likely to be depressed as those who took a vacation once every two to five years.[22]

The answer isn't for everyone to take luxury vacations. That's not possible; nor is it necessary. The needed response is for a counter-cultural approach to rest and recovery. Taking time to unplug and seek rest and recovery not only has health benefits; it also reminds us that God is God—and we are not him. We are also reminded that the world can and does continue without us.

I remember one of my seminary professors saying, "You can choose to break the Sabbath, but you will be first broken by it." Despite my respect for this professor and his wise words of caution, I chose for many years to break the Sabbath. There always seemed to be too much to do to be able to step back. It also seemed too hard to swim against the 24/7/365 current.

However, in recent years I have discovered that my choice was breaking me as well as robbing my family of a great gift. So now we seek to set one day a week aside as a Sabbath. This day is as clear of work, social media, technology, shopping and external activity as possible. Instead, our focus is being part of our local church service, taking time to rest, engaging with family and having fun. This day and rhythm have become a special gift that restores, refocuses and renews.

Being perpetually connected to social media is another significant challenge to finding rest and renewal. The constant barrage of emails, calls, posts, information and connectivity provides an endless stream of engagement and load on our systems. Many people feel a responsibility or that it's simply self-preservation to keep up on electronic communications—even if that means checking email from the first waking minute of the day during vacations.[23]

In a recent article in *Fast Company*, Baratunde Thurston, an author identified by his friends as "the most connected man in the world," reflected on his self-imposed twenty-five-day vacation and withdrawal from social media. He wrote, "The greatest gift I gave myself was a restored appreciation for disengagement, silence, and emptiness. I don't need to fill every time slot with an appointment, and I don't need to fill every mental opening with stimulus. Unoccupied moments are beautiful, so I have taken to scheduling them."[24]

Rest and renewal can be a special challenge for Christian leaders. We can view rest and renewal as laziness or wasted time. The opposite is true. As Gordon McDonald writes, "Leadership, we think, is first-class time; all other activity is second- or third-class time. Wrong! On the whole, the God of the Bible has to be just as pleased when his children play as when they work, when each is done to make possible the greater effectiveness of the other."[25]

Developing a rhythm of rest and renewal can be done simply. Some practical steps include the following:

Rest and Renewal Well Tips

- Develop some practical rhythms and commitments to a Sabbath—weekly, monthly, and yearly.

- Consider how you could punctuate your day with rhythms of rest and renewal. This could include a morning, midday and evening time of prayer or a morning workout followed by a mid-afternoon walk to re-energize.

- Aim to get the 7–8 hours of daily sleep that multiple studies conclude you do need.

- Plan vacation time a year (or at least six months) in advance. Taking a "stay-cation" or a simple vacation has many more benefits than no vacation.

- Engage in a hobby or activity that brings you life. It could be a long-lost pastime of music, art, crafts or fixing cars. Whatever it is, it can bring renewal that impacts all of your life.

- Identify clear boundaries around connectivity to technology.

Back to Aesop and the fable. The hare's arrogance shouldn't be replicated, but his approach of fully-engaged activity followed by rest and renewal is something we dismiss at our own peril.

Reflection Questions

1. Sleep, nutrition, exercise, and rest and renewal were identified as key best practices to steward physical health. With which of these are you doing well, and which are growth areas?

2. Make a list of five simple and practical application steps for your life from the ideas shared in the sections on sleeping well, eating well, exercising well, and rest and renewal.

Chapter 8

Stewardship and Shalom

People sometimes do strange things. After my first residential session as a participant in the Arrow Leadership Program, my roommate went home and made a very strange purchase. He bought 25,550 ball bearings.

The natural question is, why? Why would anyone buy 25,550 ball bearings? Well, there is a method to what may seem like my roommate's madness. The answer is profound. During that first Arrow residential session, my roommate had a transformational experience. He was deeply moved by the needs in the world. He was also awed by God's particular call on his life to be part of his mission in this chapter of history. Finally, he was convicted that God wants everyone to carefully steward their limited time on this earth. His prayer was the same as the psalmist's in Psalm 90:12: "Teach me to number my days aright so that I may gain a heart of wisdom."

So, when my roommate got back home, he took the psalmist's prayer literally. He wanted to number his days aright. To do so, he did some basic math. He estimated his lifespan to be seventy years and multiplied 70 years x 365 days. This comes out to 25,550 days of life.

Although my roommate knew that this timeframe wasn't guaranteed and that his days are ultimately held in God's hands, he was still moved by this research. He wanted to brainstorm creative ways to tangibly and visually mark this precious and finite amount of time. So, he purchased 25,550 ball bearings. With each ball bearing representing a day of his life, he counted out all the days he had already lived.

Then he put the ball bearings representing days already lived into a large jar. The rest of the ball bearings were put in another jar that represented days not yet lived. Then he began a morning ritual. Every morning he would go over to the jar of days not yet lived, pick out one ball bearing and place it in his pocket. This one ball bearing was a tangible reminder of his responsibility to steward each day that God gives him on this earth.

At the end of each day, he completed the ritual. He would take the ball bearing out of his pocket and place it in the jar representing completed days. It served as a visual reminder that each day given is a gift and resource to steward for God's glory. Once a day is gone, it is gone forever.

My Arrow roommate eventually stopped this ritual, but he recently told me that the jars still sit on his shelf as a visual reminder. This story has had a profound effect on my life. We ultimately don't know how many days we have in this life. Today could be the last one. Maybe there are thousands left. Whatever the number, this story is a vivid reminder that we are called to be stewards of this special gift of time.

The concept of stewardship is clear in Scripture. God has entrusted everyone and particularly Christian leaders with many resources—time, talent and treasure being just three. Our job is to recognize this trust as well as to seek to care for and invest these resources for God's glory.

Jesus reinforced the truth of stewardship through the parable of the talents. The master applauds the good stewardship of the servant who leveraged and maximized what was given to him. The master says, "Well done, good and faithful servant! You have been faithful with a few things; I will put you in charge of many things. Come and share in your master's happiness" (Matthew 25:21).

As followers of Christ we have been entrusted with much. As Paul writes in 1 Corinthians 4:2, "Now, it is required that those who have been given a trust must prove faithful." In other words, leading yourself well means being a steward of the trust given to you. This trust is magnified for Christian leaders who are given opportunities to leverage not only their own talents but also the talents given to others.

When I put the ball bearing illustration together with these stewardship verses, I am both convicted and inspired to wisely invest the gift of time entrusted to me. I am overwhelmed by the truth that God invites us to be part of his work and purposes. For these reasons, one of the key elements of leading ourselves is stewarding our time. But, before we get into some practical tools, it is important to note a potential danger associated with stewardship of time.

This potential danger is the temptation for stewardship to become an idol. This usually manifests itself in an insatiable drivenness toward more activity, more busyness and more accomplishment. Ironically, this kind of behavior in a leader is often applauded and encouraged by boards, churches and employers. They are impressed by and thankful for the output that often seems to accompany driven people and leaders.

However, stewardship that is hijacked by drivenness will eventually reap significant costs and casualties. In his book *Sabbath*, Wayne Muller counters the drivenness that is often behind the epidemic of busyness in North America. He writes,

> The busier we are, the more important we seem to ourselves and, we imagine, to others. To be unavailable to our friends and family, to be unable to find time for sunsets (or even to know that the sun has set at all), to whiz through our obligations without time for a mindful breath, this has become the model of a successful life.[1]

Ouch! Unfortunately, there are far too many examples of sacrifices on the altar of drivenness. We are a society that prides itself on busyness and 24/7/365 activity. In *The Rest of God*, Mark Buchanan writes that in all this frenetic activity, "the worst hallucination busyness conjures up is the conviction that I am God. All depends on me. How will the right things happen at the right time if I'm not pushing and pulling and watching and worrying?"[2]

As a result, our intimacy with God, our character, our key relationships and even our physical health can become offerings on the altar of drivenness. However, no level of achievement can compensate for some of the costs incurred.

Psalm 23 provides a beautiful corrective to the tendency toward drivenness. The reality of this psalm is that the Shepherd does not drive his sheep. Rather than pressing and demanding more and more, the Shepherd "makes me lie down in green pastures, he leads me beside quiet waters, he refreshes my soul" (Psalm 23:2–3). In other words, God is very much for our well-being and sustainability.

Another concept that expresses God's desire for our well-being is "shalom." The beautiful blessing in Numbers 6:24–26 is where we are often most familiar with the use of this word. This passage reads, "The LORD bless you and keep you; the LORD make his face shine on you and be gracious to you; the LORD turn his face toward you and give you peace [shalom]."

While usually translated as the term "peace," "shalom" is a word rich with deep meaning. It means peace, but so much more. The heart of the word means complete, perfect, full, wholeness, peace, well-being, right relationship, safety, soundness, tranquility, prosperity, fullness, rest, harmony and absence of discord. So when we share Numbers 6:24–26 as a blessing, it calls for a profound blessing of well-being on someone's entire life.

Stewardship and shalom are both God's design and intention. For God, this isn't an either-or scenario. It isn't stewardship **or** shalom. It is both. His design and desire is for Christ-followers and Christian leaders in our 24/7/365 world to live these two concepts out and to experience them simultaneously.

To develop a pathway that incorporates both stewardship and shalom, the next two chapters will look at two more key practices—leveraging your impact and managing your time.

Reflection Questions

1. How did the ball bearings story affect you? Did it inspire or discourage you?

2. Stewardship and shalom are both biblical concepts. What are your personal leadership challenges in seeking to live out both simultaneously?

3. Can you identify 2–3 action steps to help you lead yourself more effectively toward stewardship and shalom?

Chapter 9

Key Practice #5

Leveraging Your Impact

C onstruction began on the Milan Cathedral in 1386. It took six
centuries to complete this huge Gothic cathedral. Yes, it took *six*
centuries. As you enter, there are triple doorways. Above each
door is a carved symbol as well as an inscription. Over one of the doors
there is carved a beautiful wreath of roses with the inscription "All that
pleases is but for a moment." Over the second is a cross with the words
"All that troubles is but for a moment." Over the central doorway are
the words "That only is important which is eternal."[1]

These inscriptions provide a profound perspective. They challenge
us to look beyond the things that bring pleasure but for a moment. They
remind us to look beyond our many but momentary troubles. They
point us to focus on what is truly important—that which is eternal.

Putting these inscriptions alongside the story of the 25,500 ball
bearings stirs many questions. For instance, how do we focus our
short lives here on eternal things? Of all the choices and options avail-
able to many of us in North America, how do we discern God's particular call or vision for our lives? What is the greatest contribution
we can make? How do we live purposefully and make our lives
count? As Kierkegaard shared, "What I really lack is to be clear in my
mind what I am to do, not what I am to know...The thing is to understand myself, to see what God really wishes me to do...to find the
idea for which I can live and die."[2]

Each of these deep questions connects to a core theme in leading ourselves. The theme is how we leverage our impact in this life. For too many
people, even discerning what our impact should be seems like searching
for a needle in a haystack. Not only does finding clear direction seem
unattainable; knowing where to even start seems overwhelming.

However, there is some encouraging news. You actually know much more than you think about God's purpose for your life. Just look back to those four gauges from the dashboard for life in chapter 2. As a Christ-follower you already know a great deal about what God desires for you to be, to do and to steward. Right now you could likely make a long list of God's desires for you related to spiritual intimacy, your character, your relationships and your service.

You know that God desires that you enjoy a deep and vibrant relationship with him. You know that God desires that you have Christlike character evidenced by holiness, health and obedience. You know that God desires that you nurture deep and healthy relationships. You also know that God has called you to be part of his purposes and mission through service.

It is important to seek to discern the specific contribution and particular impact that God desires for you through your service or vocation. But, I encourage you to not miss the big picture of what is clear—what God has already made plain.

This leads to another important point of clarification related to God's desire for you to serve him. The clarification is summed up well in these words from Ravi Zacharias: "Because we are all priests before God, there is no distinction as 'secular or sacred.' In fact, the opposite of sacred is not secular; the opposite of sacred is profane. In short, no follower of Christ does secular work. We all have a sacred calling."[3]

For far too long a great divide has been promoted between the calling of clergy and Christian workers who serve vocationally with the Church and everybody else. Though every Christ-follower plays an important role in the mission of God, many Christians struggle to connect the dots between God's mission and their Monday to Saturday everyday lives. Some common misperceptions include the following:

- My work doesn't matter to God.

- Work is something to be endured in order to pay the bills and get closer to retirement.

- My church seems to see my ministry as only what I do when I am at church or serving in a church-run ministry. The influence and opportunities I have the rest of the week don't seem to register.

- My service to God seems limited to giving faithfully, praying when I am able and volunteering where I can in the church.

- Besides privately praying for my co-workers and trying to work with integrity, I don't see how to make a connection between my work and faith.

Vocational service in Christian ministry is a unique calling, but it is not better or worse than another kind of calling. In *Every Good Endeavor* Tim Keller supports this view. He writes, "The sixteenth-century Protestant Reformers, particularly Martin Luther and John Calvin, argued that all work, even so-called secular work, was as much a calling from God as the ministry of the monk or priest."[4]

The impact of this truth is three-fold. First, every Christ-follower should embrace the fact that God has a significant purpose for him or her in his mission. This significant purpose may be serving as a pastor who equips the saints for service. It may be as a senior corporate executive who seeks to manufacture quality goods in an environmentally sustainable way by a safe and fairly paid workforce. It may be as a homemaker who creates a safe, nurturing environment where the seeds of faith and practical life skills are prayerfully lived out and passed on day after day in the critical formative years. It may be as a farmer who labors long hours to yield a harvest to feed his own family and many others. Whatever your assignment, the bottom line is that it should not be received as a second-class assignment.

Secondly, every Christ-follower should be encouraged and enabled to proactively and intentionally discern God's calling for their life and service. The choice for those in the Western world of where and how to invest our time each week for years or even decades should not be left to circumstance or chance. It needs to be connected to God's bigger purposes, embraced as service to him, guided by a strategic approach to discernment, and celebrated through prayerful commissioning.

Third, every Christ-follower should be enabled and prayerfully supported to impact their sphere of influence for God's purposes and his glory. All of our time is God's time. This means that our service to God is not restricted to paid or volunteer hours at a local church or parachurch ministry. In other words, all twenty-four hours in our day matter to God. The forty or fifty or more hours a week many marketplace leaders invest in their jobs matter to God. Therefore, it is critical for the Church to see its purpose and impact beyond the delivery of its programs or activity within a building. The Church needs to see itself as an equipper for the rest of each week when its members are scattered in their homes, communities and workplaces.

There is another important element to consider. When we reflect on living our lives in light of eternity and leveraging our impact, we can feel a great deal of pressure. After all, we don't want to get this wrong. This leads to two temptations.

The first temptation is to believe that a bigger vision is always better. The underlying thinking is that a bigger vision is more significant because it will affect more people. Sometimes this is true, but not always.

In one of my favorite quotes, Greg Ogden provides a counter-perspective. He writes, "Jesus had enough vision to think small."[5] In other words, Jesus' intentional focus on investing deeply in only a few wouldn't be seen as a God-sized vision by many visionary leaders today. However, it wasn't a little vision. It was actually a grand vision. For in those few disciples he was preparing the future leaders of the biggest movement in the history of the world—the Church.

The takeaway point is that we shouldn't assume bigger is better. Appearances can be deceiving in God's economy. Remember the parable of the mustard seed? Jesus' story reminds us that the kingdom of God is like a tiny mustard seed that grows to become a huge plant. Our focus should be on faithful stewardship and obedience and not on trying to impress with outcomes.

A second temptation around the pressure to leverage our impact is to feel that we need to manufacture a compelling calling or vision for our lives. In his book *Me, Myself and Bob*, Phil Vischer shares how he fell into this trap. Phil was seeking to leverage his gifts as an animator and storyteller to help children connect with God's truth. His vehicle was a company he founded called VeggieTales. The key characters included animated talking vegetables, including Bob the Tomato, Larry the Cucumber and a cast of many others.

Though VeggieTales was experiencing considerable success, Phil desired to see much more. He had read Jim Collins' best-selling *Built to Last* and learned about BHAGs. BHAG is short-form for Big Hairy

Audacious Goal. Collins' argues that finding and casting a BHAG can inspire, focus and act as a catalyst for significant growth.

As Vischer reflected, he began to dream about BHAGs for VeggieTales. The BHAG he landed on was for VeggieTales to become the most trusted of the top four family entertainment companies in the world. On the surface, this sounds like a good and noble thing. After all, connecting more children to God's Word is a good and noble thing.

With this BHAG, Vischer ramped up every aspect of VeggieTales. He made key hires, added more and bigger projects, and took larger risks. Then, over time, everything fell apart. Ultimately, VeggieTales went bankrupt, many talented people lost their jobs and Vischer's dream was ruined.

This last fact is worth repeating: Vischer's dream was ruined. In the book, Vischer very transparently shares how he came to see that the BHAG was his own dream and not God's dream. Vischer realized that in his own desire and ambition to have an impact he had neglected to listen to or even ask God about his desires and plans. The result was that Vischer had leveraged everything to make an impact God wasn't asking him to make.

Leading himself, many others and his organization down this destructive road taught Vischer several hard lessons. These lessons are critical for leading ourselves in relation to our impact. The first lesson we can learn is that, as Vischer writes, "The impact God has planned for us doesn't occur when we're pursuing impact. It occurs when we're pursuing God."[6]

A second lesson we can take away is that we shouldn't try to manufacture a vision for God. Instead, we only need to seek vision from God. As Leighton Ford puts it, "Our task is not to dream up a vision for our life, but to see Jesus' vision, understand the Father's strategy for our life, and live it."[7]

It's instructive to know that Vischer's new company is called Jellyfish. He chose that name because jellyfish cannot determine their path or destination. They are guided by the currents and tides. This is a powerful and freeing reminder to all of us that God is in control and we are not.

Another reminder flowing from this story is that when God needs to communicate something specific about his vision for our lives, he does so. This revelation can come in any number of forms.

From a quick survey of the Bible, we know that this revelation can come in a whisper, a burning bush, a dream, the mouth of a donkey, a deep discontent that leads to a burden to act, an unexpected moment when we can have influence for God's purposes, the appearance of an angel, God's voice, answers to prayer, obstacles that redirect us, a sudden intervention by God, or slowly over time, as the disciples followed Jesus and were guided by the Holy Spirit.

When you look at this incomplete list, we can be assured that God doesn't use just one way to communicate his specific plans. Nor is he working on our timeline. He uses many means and his own timeline. But we can take comfort from the fact that he does communicate when we need to hear something specific.

This doesn't mean, however, that we are adrift and unaware of what God desires for us in living lives of influence. It also doesn't mean that we should just wait and do nothing. God has made a great deal very clear about his desire for our lives. So we need to seek to intentionally steward the direction and gifts he has already given to us.

One practical step you can take to steward your time and impact is to get a clearer picture of how God has wired and shaped you. In other words, you can identify the themes, strengths, gifts and talents that God has already made clear. This is simply good stewardship. As Os Guinness writes, "God normally calls us along the lines of our giftedness, but the purpose of giftedness is stewardship and service, not selfishness."[8]

The goal of doing this self-analysis is neither an inflated sense of self nor false humility. Instead, a healthy self-awareness of strengths can focus you to make your maximum contribution. As Guinness writes, "The question must now be 'How, with my existing abilities and opportunities, can I be of the greatest service to other people, knowing what I do of God's will and of human need?'"[9] This will not only make a significant kingdom difference, but stewarding strengths also brings joy.

Unfortunately, too many people simply do not know their strengths. Many others underestimate their strengths, or they don't find alignment to maximize their strengths in their work or service. The results are frustration and a significant opportunity cost from misalignment.

Spiritual gift inventories are one simple way to increase your awareness. The best inventories involve a 360-degree feedback group. This feedback will allow you to learn about gifts that others see in you. Sometimes a gift can be identified by others that you may not have seen on your own. This new insight can open up avenues of new possibility. Your responses may also be confirmed by the feedback group's perceptions. This can provide affirmation and give added confidence in leveraging your impact.

Rick Warren's SHAPE is another helpful self-awareness tool. This acronym stands for Spiritual Gifts, Heart, Abilities, Personality, and Experiences. As you work through each letter of the acronym you begin to get a bigger, fuller and clearer picture of your unique purpose.

There are many other assessments and inventories designed to increase your self-awareness. These can range from complex and specialized personality-based assessment to off-the-shelf inventories like StrengthsFinder. Though some are better than others, I find that simply taking the reflection time required is one of the best benefits.

I'm also careful to not take these inventories too far. For instance, just because an inventory says something doesn't mean it's always true. What an inventory says also isn't an excuse; nor does it mean that I'm stuck that way. Whatever an assessment says, our goal is Christlikeness. We always want to be moving in that direction. And, thankfully, the Holy Spirit can override what may be natural tendencies when needed.

Another great tool involves, strangely enough, tic-tac-toe. My executive coach shared this simple but profound tool to help me discern and steward my unique impact. It starts with drawing a tic-tac-toe grid on a blank piece of paper. The second step is to fill each of the nine empty boxes with a word or phrase that describes you at your best as it relates to serving, working and doing. These nine words or phrases describe your best contribution through what you already know about your passion, skills, abilities, gifts, experiences, and environment.

Unlike tic-tac-toe there is no strategic arrangement of the contents of the boxes. But when you do get all nine filled in with a key word or phrase, you will have a fairly descriptive picture of you at your best for maximum impact and effective service.

To give you an example, my tic-tac-toe box would include these words and phrases: teach, mentor/coach, write/create resources, ambassador, Christian leaders, strategic difference, travel, lead and shepherd.

When I'm investing time in these nine ways, I feel alive and aligned with God's call on my life. They are me at my best, making my best contribution and leveraging my best impact.

Each of these nine words are unique to me. You will very likely have very different words, and this is good! These nine words are also unique to this stage of my life. Fifteen years ago, some of the words would have been very different, and I anticipate that fifteen years from now the list will be different too.

Some words in my list are more important than others. God seems to have woven some of these words into my life long ago and some more recently. I've been encouraged because the community of God's people has affirmed these words over time as priorities for my life. As with all things, though, God has the ultimate veto and direction in my life. He can change these words as he shapes me and calls me.

To apply this simple tool, you can compare each of your nine boxes against your current setting for service. To do this, get three colored pencils or pens—red, yellow and green. As you compare each ideal box to your current setting, circle it with the corresponding color. Red is for a poor match. In other words, you aren't really able to live this out in your current context. Yellow isn't ideal but is okay or has possibility for improvement. Green means that you are able to live this out regularly in your context.

It's unlikely that all nine of your boxes will be "green" all the time. There are also some aspects of every role that we just need to embrace and do. However, if a majority of these boxes are not green most of the time, you will very likely experience frustration, stress and fatigue. If this is your situation, you can reflect on what you can change about your context. Is there anything you can do that will allow you to spend more time working from these nine words? Can some activities be stopped or delegated? Can you better prioritize and guard some of these words?

You could also share your tic-tac-toe chart with your supervisor. You need to do this wisely and carefully, but your goal is to help your supervisor leverage the best from you. By sharing you at your best from the chart and where your current role has some stress or stretch points, you can engage your supervisor's help. Maybe your role can be adjusted in a way that allows more emphasis on these nine areas. Maybe there is another role within the organization that would be a better fit.

Barring God's redirection, you may conclude that you need to change your work setting in order to better leverage you at your best. If this is the case, the tic-tac-toe tool is also a great help in considering new opportunities. It provides a simple objective filter to evaluate new possible roles rather than being overwhelmed by all the different possibilities. As you learn more about a new role, you can evaluate whether each box is red, yellow or green. Unless God clearly leads you otherwise, you shouldn't accept a new role where most boxes are not green.

The last tool I will share is a personal vision statement. This statement is a compilation of what you already know about yourself combined with who God is calling you to be and what you do know he has called you to do. Notice that I'm talking about *you*. Your calling and vision statement will be unique to you. This should be a freeing reality. Os Guinness writes, "When Jesus calls, he calls us one by one. Comparisons are idle, speculations about others a waste of time, and envy as silly as it is evil. We are each called individually, accountable to God alone, to please him alone and eventually to be approved by him alone."[10]

This means that we shouldn't be like Peter during his reinstatement by Jesus. When Jesus called Peter to "Take care of my sheep" (John 21:16), Peter saw "that the disciple whom Jesus loved was following them" (v. 20). So Peter asked, "Lord, what about him?" (v. 21). Jesus' response is instructive to all of us: "What is that to you? You must follow me" (v. 22). In other words, don't worry about what God asks others to do. Instead, be faithful in what God asks you to do.

A personal vision statement acts like a compass. It doesn't necessarily tell you the next step, but it does orient you to the right direction for your life. It takes some time, prayerful reflection and work to develop a written statement. It also takes some upkeep with reflection and revisions as life changes.

There's a tendency to exclusively focus on our work, service or doing in a personal vision statement. I would encourage you to think holistically. God wants you to be fully transformed and focused on his purposes in all aspects of your life. So paint the whole big picture of your calling in a personal vision statement. This means that your statement will include sections on spiritual intimacy, character, relationships and service.

To develop a personal vision statement, there are some key ingredients required. For starters, seeking to be intentional in this way requires openness. As you seek greater clarity from God, you need to be open to however he responds. This process very well may lead you outside your comfort zone and challenge you to obedience in the face of change.

A second key ingredient is spiritual discipline. Discernment of your personal vision is first and foremost a spiritual activity. You cannot minimize or compromise on actively seeking the Lord's direction through solitude, prayer, fasting and waiting. Ask the Lord in prayer to more clearly and fully reveal his direction for your life. Listen for the Lord in times of solitude and fasting.

Time is another key ingredient. While the Lord can and sometimes does reveal things in an instant, this process may take significant time in reflection, prayer, waiting, discernment, formulation, wordsmithing, refinement, etc. Patience and intentionality in setting apart time are important for the discernment process. As St. Vincent de Paul is believed to have said, "He who is in a hurry delays the things of God."

The Lord often seems to operate on a first-things-first basis. This means that he wants us to deal with blockages, hindrances and obedience issues before he gives us more insight or responsibility. This requires you to ask if there is any "business" in the form of spiritual bungee cords or issues of obedience that the Lord would desire you to resolve. Pray, ask and listen.

Another key ingredient to this process is community. The body of Christ can provide prayer support, discernment, encouragement, affirmation and accountability as you seek the Lord's direction. Do you know godly people whom you trust to "seek first his kingdom and his righteousness" (and not their own agenda or your agenda) and who could serve in these roles on your behalf and on behalf of the community of Christ? If so, invite these people to be a sounding board and help you develop your personal vision statement.

A template to craft a personal vision statement is located in appendix A.

Reflection Questions

1. How do you see your vocation as part of God's mission?

2. One key element of leveraging your impact is identifying the themes, strengths, gifts and talents that God has already made clear in your life. If you didn't do so already, go back and do the tic-tac-toe exercise. What are your nine words or phrases? Does anything surprise you about this list? How does your tic-tac-toe list align with your current vocation?

3. What would need to change for you to invest more time and energy in leveraging your strengths, gifts and vision?

4. Have you developed a personal vision statement in the past? If so, review and update it. If not, you can get started by reviewing the template in the appendix.

Chapter 10

Key Practice #6

Managing Your Time

In his classic book *The Effective Executive*, management guru Peter Drucker writes about time. His first of three insights is that time is inelastic. In other words, it cannot be stretched or stored. Each perishable second ticks by and is gone forever. Drucker's second insight is that time is irreplaceable. Once used, it cannot be reclaimed. We can't will it back; nor can we buy it back. When it is gone, it is gone. His third characteristic is that time is indispensable. This means that we can't do anything without it. We need time for everything.[1]

Managing this inelastic, irreplaceable and indispensable resource is foundational for leading yourself well. Managing your time is a stewardship issue. Stewarding your time pleases God and keeps you focused on his purposes for your life.

In addition, if you manage your time well, you will have a much greater chance of accomplishing what you need to accomplish while experiencing shalom. All of this leaves a really big and important question— how do you do it?

The first step requires some new paradigms. Three key paradigm shifts are related to time.

Paradigm Shift #1—We are heirs of eternity, not short of days

In *The Rest of God* Mark Buchanan writes, "Most of us live afraid that we're almost out of time. But you and I, we're heirs of eternity. We're not short of days. We just need to number them right."[2] This truth that Christ-followers are heirs of eternity seems to take some of the pressure off somehow. Remembering back to the example of the 25,500 ball bearings, we all have a limited supply of ball bearings in this life, but there's an eternal supply of ball bearings when we run out.

Paradigm Shift #2—Focus on making your dent, not saving the world

Gordon MacDonald provides another paradigm-shifting thought. In *Building Below the Waterline* he writes, "Slowly we learn that we cannot save the world, but rather, we can make a dent on our world."[3] This is a good challenge to those of us who feel called to save the world and lean toward stewardship rather than shalom. Focusing on just making my "dent" helps keep shalom in a healthy tension with stewardship.

MacDonald goes on to share,

> I now reject what I feel is the superficial intensity of much Christian ministry: that everything is a problem, that every person needs to be fixed, and that all the work of the kingdom has to be done by the time I die. Ministry is my life, but I am no longer reluctant to make sure there is time on my calendar (with family and friends).[4]

When I think about my own drivenness and I look for things that draw me away from shalom, it's this one. Part of this driveness roots back to my distorted vision of God, and part is rooted in the idea that if I don't do it, or if it doesn't get done today, tomorrow or in my lifetime, it won't be done. I would have been deeply frustrated if I had worked on the Milan Cathedral, knowing I would never see its completion. For me, this paradigm shift is about recognizing that God is on the throne from beginning to end. He is working out his timing for the world. He is "from everlasting to everlasting" (Psalm 90:2), and I can trust him to accomplish his work in his timing.

Paradigm Shift #3—Patience rather than frantic hurrying about

I get frustrated waiting for virtually anything. I like to see quick action and immediate forward movement. However, I am slowly learning that even waiting and delays can be gifts.

Ironically, many people in North America pride themselves on their level of busyness and hurry. We even begin conversations with the question "Are you keeping busy?" as if keeping busy was a good thing. There's a wise saying in Swahili, "*Haraka haraka haina baraka.*" This means "Hurry, hurry has no blessings."

Beyond these three paradigm shifts, there are also some very practical tools that you can leverage to effectively manage your time. This next section will provide eleven tips to help you lead yourself well as you steward time.

Tip #1—Identify and Prioritize Your Big Rocks

The first tool is based around Stephen Covey's powerful parable about the big rocks. Covey's original story is shared by one of his associates:

> I attended a seminar once where the instructor was lecturing on time. At one point, he said, "Okay, it's time for a quiz." He reached under the table and pulled out a wide-mouth gallon jar. He set it on the table next to a platter with some fist-sized rocks on it. "How many of these rocks to do you think we can get into the jar?" he asked.
>
> After we made our guess, he said, "Okay. Let's find out." He set one rock in the jar...then another...then another. I don't remember how many he got in, but he got the jar full. Then he asked, "Is that jar full?"
>
> Everybody looked at rocks and said, "Yes."
>
> Then he said, "Ahhh." He reached under the table and pulled out a bucket of gravel. Then he dumped some gravel in and shook the jar and the gravel went into the little spaces left by the big rocks. Then he grinned and said once more, "Is the jar full?"
>
> By this time we were on to him. "Probably not," we said.
>
> "Good!" he replied. And he reached under the table and brought out a bucket of sand. He started dumping the sand in and it went in all the little space left the rocks and the gravel. Once more he looked at us and said, "Is the jar full?"
>
> "No!" we all roared.
>
> He said, "Good!" and he grabbed a pitcher of water and began to pour it in. He got something like a quart of water in that jar. Then he said, "Well, what's the point?"
>
> Somebody said, "Well, there are gaps, and if you really work at it, you can always fit more into your life."
>
> "No," he said, "that's not the point. The point is this: if you hadn't put these big rocks in first, would you ever have gotten any of them in?"[5]

Covey's classic illustration is a great teacher about priorities. The objective isn't to cram as much into your "jar" or life as possible. The key is to identify the "big rocks" and make sure they get in first. Everything else follows.

Applied to time, this means you need to identify your most important priorities and make sure they are given priority. The simple question "What are your big rocks?" helps you identify priorities that need to take precedence over other less important things.

The big-rocks concept can be applied at several levels of your life. For starters, if you apply this concept to your life overall, your big rocks closely relate to the key elements from your personal vision statement. This connects you back to the dashboard and the key dimensions of spiritual intimacy, character, relationships and service that you are seeking to prioritize and steward. These big rocks need to take priority as you manage your time.

To identify the big rocks for your work year, look at the key objectives of the organization and the key deliverables for your role. A conversation with your supervisor and team as well as your own self-awareness around your greatest contribution will bring you even greater clarity. These big rocks then need to take priority in your schedule as you manage your time.

To apply this tool weekly, you can simply ask yourself on Sunday night, "What are the big rocks for this next week?" This means discerning which deadlines, outcomes and people need to be prioritized in your time. Once you identify these big rocks, you should ensure that they are clearly defined in your daily calendar. If these are the most important things, your time needs to be allocated and guarded to accomplish them.

You can also use this tool with your team. You can have a ten-minute stand-up meeting with your team on Monday morning. Ask each team member to share their big rocks for the week. This not only will help them to focus but also will help the team leader to know how to help or when to redirect someone to more important big rocks. It's also useful for team members to know what others are working on in case they can help or are needed to help.

Lack of clarity around big rocks can drain energy and lead to feelings of confusion or being overwhelmed. Just the opposite is true when you have clarity around big rocks. Clarity around your big rocks should stir your energy and excitement.

Tip #2—Plan One Year Out

This tool applies the big-rocks concept one step further. Too often leaders live in a frantic short-term horizon of competing demands. Planning out one year in advance can help ensure that "big rocks" will receive focus and will also highlight potential pressure points during the year. Executive coach Bobb Biehl[6] shares a unique way to do this using the template of a clock. Here are the six key steps:

Step 1—Get a large piece of paper and draw a big clock-type circle on it.

Step 2—Mark the hours on the clock with the months of the year—not with the usual numbers (i.e., January instead of 1, December instead of 12, etc.).

Step 3—Use different colored markers to mark on the clock what you already know about the year ahead. For example, use one color to mark all the personal events you know about on the calendar—birthdays, anniversaries, holidays, etc. Go back with another color to put on all non-negotiable events—board meetings, key school gatherings, major work trips or responsibilities, etc.

Step 4—Now look at your big rocks. Mark your big rocks in different colors. For example, put personal big rocks in one color. Put team and organizational big rocks in different colors.

Step 5—Step back and take a look at the clock. Where are the pressure points? In other words, where is there too much activity? Can you shift any items to quieter times? Can you add any rest and family time before or after the busy seasons? Have you factored in preparation time? You may discover that you need to make some changes at this step to avoid being overwhelmed later in the year.

Step 6—Post your year clock somewhere where you can see it. Consult this calendar before you make major commitments during the year. Update and review regularly.

Tip #3—Find Balcony Time

Just as stage directors or football coaches sometimes move to the balcony or press box for some fresh perspective, leaders can benefit from regular times of pulling back and looking at things from a wider and different angle.

Jesus took time away. He had a rhythm of pulling back, listening to God and processing things from a wider and different angle. Jesus was clearly gifted and had endless demands on his time. Yet he was able to hold stewardship and shalom together. One key reason was because he knew his calling and his priorities. This informed his overarching impact and his day-to-day activities.

In Mark 1:35, Jesus pulled away from the crowds and the chaos and spent time with God. When Simon and his companions found him, they exclaimed, "Everyone is looking for you!" (v. 37). People had great plans and demands for Jesus. Yet Jesus kept his course. He emerged from this balcony time with great clarity and resolve. He had discerned that he shouldn't stay put. He needed to move on, so he said, "Let us go somewhere else—to the nearby villages—so I can preach there also. That is why I have come" (v. 38).

Finding your balcony space is important. It's where you can pull away, reflect without distraction, pray and see things from a different perspective. This may be going to a coffee shop or a retreat center with your journal; it may be a daily walk around your neighborhood; or it could be taking a road trip with some colleagues to a conference or to visit another organization. Regardless, you need to have regular balcony time experiences to gain the perspective needed to better steward your time every day.

Tip #4—Create a Parking Lot

If you are an idea person you need a place to store or "park" your ideas so they aren't lost and so they don't distract you or others. These distractions can consume valuable time in meetings or as you process in your head when you should be doing other things.

This "parking lot" can be a journal, whiteboard or special file folder. When a great idea that doesn't require immediate attention comes to mind, write it down and know that it is safely stored for future reference. Then you can get back on focus and task.

The parking lot concept is also great tool for helping meetings stay on track. If a great idea or an interesting issue is raised that's not on the agenda, then acknowledge the contribution by writing it down on the list of parking lot items for later discussion. It respects the contributor, guards the ideas from being lost and keeps you from getting sidetracked!

Tip #5—Make Appointments With Yourself

We make appointments for many things—trips to the dentist, coffee with a friend, meetings, and much more. But we rarely make appointments with ourselves. Guarding time for yourself is worthy of an appointment. The purpose of self-appointments can be to prepare for a project, to read, to reflect, to think, to rest or to exercise. Treat these appointments with the same respect you have for appointments with other people. When someone asks you to meet at a certain time when you've already got an appointment booked to review your big rocks for the year, you can suggest an alternate time because you already have an appointment.

One last thought about appointments with yourself. Never cancel these appointments; only reschedule.

Tip #6—Use Filters

Filters are designed to separate. Your coffeemaker allows hot water to mix with the coffee grounds, but the filter delivers hot coffee free of crunchy coffee grounds. The same concept is a helpful tool for managing your time. If you have multiple voices demanding your time, you need to have some filters. These filters allow you time and space to discern which demands or requests match your calling and priorities. These filters help you to say "yes," and they help you to know when to say "no" or "not now."

For example, your organization's mission statement and your personal vision statement are both filters. If your mission is manufacturing but this opportunity is about a new human resources business, your mission statement can help you filter this out and avoid spending more time on research and deliberations.

Similarly, if you have an assistant, he or she can act as a filter for phone calls, emails and drop-in appointments. If you share your tic-tac-toe chart and big rocks lists with your assistant, he or she can help keep your time focused on these core activities.

Identifying specific planning windows can be another helpful filter. For instance, instead of getting sidetracked and distracted by a new idea, invitation or opportunity, you can "park" it until your next scheduled planning time. This can both save time now and help you make a better decision when the time is right.

Tip #7—Try Working in Shorter Bursts

Sometimes you can get overwhelmed looking at a big project. As a result, you keep procrastinating or decide to wait for a big block of time—which is often hard to find. Don't underestimate the value and potential impact of short bursts of time. For instance, if you are overwhelmed at the disarray in your home or office, set a timer for 15 minutes and get cleaning or organizing. You will not only be surprised at how much you can get done, you may also find new energy to keep going.

Similarly, if you set aside a solid hour or ninety minutes for a burst of effort toward a big project, you can often get more accomplished than you would think. If you can put this hour into a regular rhythm (daily or weekly), you will experience regular progress. I've often experienced that I can accomplish much more than I expect in an hour and less than I expect in a day.

Tip #8—Find Your Best Rhythm

Are you sharper in the morning, afternoon or evening? Managing your time well means identifying when you are at your best and carefully scheduling this time for maximum impact.

Too many people start each day reacting to immediate needs and distractions. For most people, this means responding to other people's needs that have collected overnight via email. This usually starts an entire day that is spent reacting to other people's big rocks or needs.

The anecdote is to schedule yourself to maximize yourself at your best. For instance, I'm sharpest and most creative in the morning. This means that I try to schedule one or two ninety-minute blocks of time in the morning for writing, thinking or working on my own. Then I schedule meetings and can pick up energy from connections with people. Mid-afternoon, I try to take a 15 to 20 minute walk. This brief exercise recharges my batteries and refocuses my thoughts so I can finish the day strong.

Whatever your rhythm, you should try to be proactive about scheduling your time. Depending on your context, this can include a daily, weekly, or monthly routine. This routine can also help free you from the tyranny of ever-changing to-do lists.

Tip #9—Say No

To lead yourself well you need to be able to say no. Peter Drucker said, "People are effective because they say 'no,' because they say, 'this isn't for me.'"[7] Saying no isn't easy for many of us. We want to help, to please, to contribute and to be needed. However, leading yourself well means keeping focused on the mission, roles and tasks God has called you to steward. This means saying no sometimes—saying no to taking on new assignments, saying no to distractions, saying no to your own desires and saying no to other people who want to make their crisis your emergency.

An important note of caution accompanies this time-management tip: Be sure you are listening to God and allowing the Holy Spirit to guide you. Jesus' days very often included what seemed like interruptions or distractions. At face value, on his mission to save the world, being asked to heal one leper, deal with one demon- possessed man or chat with one tax collector seems like an interruption or distraction. However, through listening to and depending on the Holy Spirit, he saw many of these interruptions as God-ordained appointments. Jesus' overarching focus was to live in complete obedience to the Father's call on his life. Very often this meant being sensitive to unscheduled opportunities and responsibilities.

Tip #10—Delegate to and Develop Others

Jethro provided his son-in-law Moses with some valuable correction. After watching Moses spend a day serving as a judge for the people, he said, "What you are doing is not good. You and these people who come to you will only wear yourselves out. The work is too heavy for you; you cannot handle it alone" (Exodus 18:17–18).

Jethro instructed Moses to, instead of doing it all on his own, identify others who were qualified and delegate responsibility and authority to them. Jethro said, "But select capable men from all the people—men who fear God, trustworthy men who hate dishonest gain—and appoint them officials over thousands, hundreds, fifties and tens" (Exodus 18:21).

Through delegation, Moses would empower others to serve, provide more timely responses to the people and free himself up from carrying the entire load as the lone judge. By delegating, Moses would be able to use his limited time to do other important things. This is a win-win-win scenario. It seems like a no-brainer. Yet many people struggle with delegation.

The struggle to delegate is rooted in some common concerns. For starters, there's the concern about quality. After all, what if the job's not done as well as I could do it or need it done? There are also fears. For instance, what if someone else does this better than me? There are also practical arguments, like it's faster to do it myself than to train someone else and delegate.

Bobb Biehl puts these concerns in perspective. One of his wise adages is "When you are doing something that someone else on your staff could do 80% as well, you are probably wasting your time doing it."[8] Biehl's point is that there is an opportunity cost to everything you do. If you choose to do one thing, you can't do another. His point is to identify the few things that only you can do and do them really well. At the same time, you need to develop others and delegate as much of everything else as possible. Even if they don't do it 100 percent as well as you do, in most cases 80 percent is still more than adequate. This frees you up to focus on what only you can do and empowers others at the same time.

There are many good resources to help you grow in this area. Here are three tips to get you started:

1. **Clarify What You Are Delegating**—Are you delegating a *task* or a *project* or a *function*? You need to have greater levels of confidence moving from delegating tasks to projects to functions. This confidence can be earned as people prove faithful over time with growing levels of responsibility.

2. **Clarify Outcomes**—Communicate clearly about the specific deliverables or outcomes that you expect. Leave room for the individuals to determine their own process or chart their own course. But make the target of success crystal clear.

3. **Reflection, Learning and Celebration**—Close the loop through an intentional debrief of the delegation experience. Take time appropriate to the person's experience and the complexity of what was delegated to reflect, learn and, hopefully, celebrate.

Tip #11—Stop Trying to Multitask

There's a popular idea that you can accomplish more by multitasking. After all, it does seem more efficient to do multiple things at once. Plus, it can seem energizing to have more than one thing on the go at the same time.

Though this idea about multitasking is popular, it simply isn't true. In fact, research shows that "Multitasking is not efficient, nor does it get more work done faster. Quite the opposite. One task interferes with another, so everything takes longer because the brain loses time—and accuracy — in repeatedly shifting its effort."[9]

So in reality multitasking is inefficient. For starters, it's slower and less accurate. The constant information load also prevents downtime for the brain, which slows or prevents learning and memory retention.[10] It's also quite costly. Studies show that the average worker loses 2.1 hours per day due to unnecessary interruptions—costing the economy an estimated $650 billion per year.[11]

This doesn't mean that we can never do two things at once. But it does mean we can't effectively do more than one thing at once that requires focus. So, a surgeon can listen to music in the operating theatre and still effectively focus on the operation at hand. Listening to music in the background doesn't require focus or detract from focus on the operation. What the surgeon can't do effectively is focus on the operation and try to focus on or switch between other tasks. You don't want a surgeon who is checking his or her email in the operating room. It is much more efficient (and, in this case, safe) to focus on one task at a time. The more switching between tasks, the slower and less efficient you are.

Reflection Questions

1. What paradigm shift do you need to make related to time?

2. If you could free up an hour of time each day, how would you spend it?

3. What changes do you want to make to manage your time more effectively?

Chapter 11

Key Practice #7
Dealing with Dandelions

Dandelions. These yellow weeds temporarily disguised as flowers populate lawns in North America each spring. Initially, it seems easiest to just run the lawnmower over top of them. After all, they will disappear...for a day or two.

Their disappearance is very temporary. They will return in even greater force. As someone who has tried the lawnmower approach (more than once), I have learned that the only way to truly eliminate dandelions is to get to the roots with some sort of nasty poison or a back-breaking weeding tool.

Getting to the roots of dandelions has a profound application to leading yourself. Too often we try to tackle struggles and negative behaviors in our lives without addressing the root issues below the surface. Instead, we try a quick-fix solution. We may even get some initial positive benefit and results. Things may seem different temporarily. But, before long, the same old behavior appears again.

Initially, the most common response is to buckle down and try harder. Sometimes this can mean trying harder spiritually. We try to read more Scripture, pray more or go to more church functions. Although reading Scripture, praying and engaging with church are positive behaviors, trying to do them better or more often might not get down to the roots of your specific issue. Trying harder may be like choosing to cut the lawn more often. The dandelions disappear more frequently, but they keep popping up. Then, frustration sets in.

This frustration can occur on a number of levels. You can become frustrated with God. You can feel that he is distant, disinterested or not powerful enough to help you overcome your challenge. You can also get frustrated with yourself. Falling back into the same old behavior can bring feelings of guilt and shame and even a sense that you are beyond help. Finally, the people and community around you can become the focus of your frustration. Since you are trying hard, you might surmise that your lack of progress must be connected to the people around you. So it's tempting to put the blame on their perceived lack of care, support or resources.

In reality, your approach may be the problem. You've simply taken the lawnmower to your dandelions. Maybe you've determined to stop or start a behavior, and you may even have a clear new plan to learn and move forward. However, if you've neglected to address the roots below the surface that are continuing to support the behaviors and patterns you are trying to overcome, frustration is the likeliest outcome.

Harvard professors Robert Kegan and Lisa Laskow Lahey call these roots "competing commitments" in their book *Immunity to Change*. These competing commitments are the beliefs or behaviors that we engage in or don't engage in that work against a desired change. These competing commitments are rooted in assumptions that we've made and desire to protect. Similar to the antibodies that fight against an attacking virus in our bodies, competing commitments fight against change—even if it is good or desired—in order to protect our assumptions and more comfortable status quo.

Here's an example. Say someone wants to lose weight and get into better shape. Some common first steps would include learning more about healthy nutrition, joining a gym and finding some friends to keep the person accountable. These are all good and practical steps.

However, imagine that, despite some initial weight loss, the person has actually gained weight despite knowing much more about healthy nutrition and exercise. Interestingly, this scenario is not farfetched. Research indicates that the average dieter returns to 107 percent of their original weight.[1] Ironically, this means they weigh 7 percent more after they diet.

Clearly, someone who wants to get into better shape and is taking practical steps to do so would be frustrated by actually getting farther away from their goal. The key question is, why? Why are they taking backward steps?

The answer to this question could very likely be rooted in a competing commitment. For example, suppose this person is working in a role outside their skillset. Because they are working outside their skillset, they have difficulty completing projects on time or to the level required. Stress is the outcome. As this stress builds, the person seeks comfort. This comfort is found in junk food. So, even though they want to get into better shape and they are taking positive steps to do so, they eat more and more junk food. They do this because it provides a comfort and stress reliever. The results are a lack of positive change in health and a growing frustration.

Deepening knowledge and growing skills are important. Sometimes these steps are the best course of action. But these steps fall short when deeper issues exist. These deeper issues are "competing commitments," and, like dandelions, they often have roots below the surface. These roots are beliefs held or behaviors that support your assumptions. They also reinforce the status quo while fighting against the desired change.

In this scenario there are at least two competing commitments. The first is the behavior of eating junk food to relieve work-related stress. The second is avoidance of a potentially difficult conversation with the manager. Both of these competing commitments are based on some assumptions. The first assumption is that eating junk food is actually the only or best way to relieve stress. The second assumption may be the belief that this work situation is unchangeable or that the manager doesn't care, or a fear related to potential conflict that could arise with the manager.

To get traction on your desired change, you need to identify the competing commitments and then probe as well as challenge the assumptions that support them. The outcome of this process is making a new commitment that adapts your mindset as well as identifying clear first steps. Next steps include identifying some markers that would indicate significant progress and ultimate success.

In this example, the assumptions behind the competing commitments need to be challenged. Specifically, the assumption that junk food is the best way to relieve stress can't be true in light of the stress resulting from not getting in or being in better physical health. The assumption that the work situation is unchangeable is also questionable. The employee doesn't know this without a doubt because they have avoided having a potentially difficult conversation with their manager.

Challenging the assumptions behind competing commitments is not easy. In fact, it will stir fears and all sorts of negative thinking. This is when you feel the immunity to change pushing back and trying to maintain the status quo.

The good news is that a new commitment to grow in physical health by addressing workplace stress can be made with one clear first step. This first step should be to explore the work-related stress concerns with the manager. After all, maybe the manager isn't even aware of the stress. Maybe there are some easy adjustments that can be made to the employee's role. Maybe more training could grow the employee's skills to greater proficiency. Making a new commitment and taking some first steps are crucial to beginning to make forward progress.

Outlining significant progress markers is also critical. These progress markers are new behaviors and responses that help you know you are moving in the right direction. For instance, one progress marker could be making a different response when work stressors arise. Maybe the progress marker is choosing to go to the gym to work off the stress. Or it could be choosing to have a proactive conversation with the manager before stress mounts.

Finally, it's important to map out a picture of success. What would success look like? In this example, success would be reduced stress at work, healthy responses to stress and better overall physical health.

Jesus and Competing Commitments

Kegan and Lahey weren't the first to understand the concept of immunity to change or the importance of addressing competing commitments. Jesus was a master at getting past the surface issues and helping people identify their competing commitments. Think about the rich man in Mark 10. He was desperate to know the answer to one of life's biggest questions. He ran to Jesus, fell to his knees and said, "Good teacher…what must I do to inherit eternal life?" (Mark 10:17).

Jesus responded with a question: "Why do you call me good?…No one is good—except God alone" (Mark 10:18). This may have been Jesus' way of getting at the rich man's competing commitments and assumptions. In effect, Jesus was saying, "Before I answer your question, I want to know if you will be accepting my answer. That depends on whether or not you respect me as the source of authority for your life. If you don't, it doesn't matter what I say."

As the conversation continues, the man attests to his faithfulness in keeping the commandments. The story continues with one of my favorite verses from Scripture: "Jesus looked at him and loved him" (Mark 10:21).

Here's how Jesus loved him. He said, "One thing you lack...Go, sell everything you have and give it to the poor, and you will have treasure in heaven. Then come, follow me" (Mark 10:21). In loving this man, Jesus was not condemning his wealth or adding more external behavioral changes by commanding generous giving. What Jesus was doing was powerfully pointing out that a deeper internal change is required for eternal life. Jesus was highlighting the man's competing commitments.

By telling him to sell everything, Jesus was pointing out that the man's security and identity were in his material wealth. These assumptions were actually impeding him as he pursued his desired goal. True security and identity are only found in Christ.

Jesus was also pointing out another competing commitment of profound theological significance. Despite his faithful adherence to the commandments and his desire to "do" what it took to inherit eternal life, the rich man was incapable of earning grace. He needed to come to Christ with nothing, because there is nothing any of us can offer God for our salvation.

When faced with his competing commitments, the rich man's immunity to change likely kicked into high gear. It began to fight against the change and fight for the status quo. If we could have heard the chatter in his brain, we might have heard him saying, "If I sell everything and give it away, how will I live? What about my standing in the community? Surely all my good works will suffice in pleasing God. How can I be sure that I can really trust this teacher?" Well, we know the rest of the story. "At this the man's face fell. He went away sad, because he had great wealth" (Mark 10:22).

Applying the concept of competing commitments has helped me forge several breakthroughs in my own life. For years I struggled with conflict. If you asked me to play the word association game with the word "conflict," my words wouldn't be positive. I've had an allergy to conflict my entire life. Like the majority of ministry leaders, I've sought to avoid it—sometimes at great cost.

Some people attributed my conflict avoidance to positive characteristics. They would say that I'm gentle, diplomatic or good at peacemaking. But I've known better. For the most part, I wasn't mastering conflict; it was mastering me. My attempts to avoid conflict left me frustrated at myself. I got frustrated when I didn't speak up, defend or share something important. I also got frustrated when I watched what would have been a smaller conflict if it had been addressed early on become something much bigger, messier and unavoidable later on. I'm sure my allergy to conflict also frustrated others who wanted me to speak my mind or take quicker action on some issues.

I knew that this pattern wasn't healthy—particularly for a leader involved with leading people and organizations. I also knew that my approach wasn't biblical. For one, Jesus didn't always avoid conflict. Sometimes he very intentionally stirred up or engaged in conflict. So, I knew I *needed* to see change in this area of my life. I also *wanted* to see change in this area of my life.

My first step toward change was knowledge- and skill-based. I decided to learn more about conflict and related skills. Thankfully, there are many helpful resources on conflict—books like *Difficult Conversations, Fierce Conversations* and *Crucial Conversations*. I read these along with other books and took notes along the way.

I also discovered the Thomas Kilmann Inventory. Through this tool I discovered that there are more ways to approach conflict than avoidance. In addition to avoiding, they identify accommodating, compromising, collaborating and competing as distinct conflict styles. I also learned that different situations require different conflict styles. So, rather than going to my default, I began to ask myself which style was best in different scenarios.

All of this learning was very practical and very helpful. I was making some progress. I would try to approach conflict situations differently. However, I kept defaulting back to my old approach. This became frustrating, and after a while I began to sense that there was something deeper that needed to be addressed. More knowledge and skill development were helpful in many ways, but it was like running a lawnmower over the dandelions. It worked for a few days, but the dandelions popped back up. I wasn't getting to the roots. It was becoming clear that changing my approach to conflict wasn't about learning more or trying harder. It would require a deeper internal change.

Without knowing where to turn, I brought this issue to my coach. She suggested that I write down everything I believed about conflict. She encouraged me to write my beliefs without a filter. In other words, she wanted me to write what I currently believed and to try not to think about what I *should* think about conflict.

I took on this assignment and began to write. Before long, I wrote down the words "Conflict hurts people." I had surprised myself by even writing these words. I didn't really know where they had come from, but they had come. And when I wrote them, I knew that this belief was deep and powerful.

After I finished my list of beliefs, my coach encouraged me to go back over my list. She wanted me to explore where each belief came from and to try to discern whether or not the belief was both biblical and healthy.

As I went back through my list, it all started to come together. My early years had been lived in the midst of conflict. My mom struggled with mental illness, prescription drug abuse and alcoholism. On some days she was a fantastic mom, and on others our home was embroiled in conflict. It was during these conflicts that I would try to do whatever I could to facilitate the absence of conflict or bring peace. It was then that I became a conflict avoider.

I already knew that we're all shaped both positively and negatively by our families and growing-up years. I had already made some of these connections to my adult life. But, I had overlooked one key area. Actually, I had overlooked one key event. It was during the Christmas holidays when I was in grade six. The conflict and turmoil in my family had reached a crisis point. Our family was separating. I remember as an eleven-year-old looking my mom in the eyes and, in whatever words I put together, telling her that the separation was needed and that I felt I should leave with my dad and sister.

It's a memory that can still put a lump in my throat. That moment hurt everyone involved. It was also when I resolved that "conflict hurts people." This belief became my competing commitment. I didn't want to engage in conflict, even when conflict was healthy and important. My assumption was that conflict deeply hurt people, and I didn't want any part of hurting others.

With this new insight, I took a number of first steps forward. First, I sought God's healing for the hurt that began that day. God can and does heal our wounds from the past. Sometimes this is instant, and sometimes it occurs over time. Regardless, I can depend on God's healing hand and ongoing help as I seek holiness and wholeness.

Second, I asked God's forgiveness for years of approaching conflict from the perspective of how it impacted me rather than seeking his kingdom purposes. We are not designed to approach life from the compass of our preferences or comfort. Instead, we are to pursue Matthew 6:33, where Jesus says, "But seek first his kingdom and his righteousness."

Third, I declared and embraced the truths that conflict is part of this life and that conflict can be redemptive. In my case, I made a list of the results that can come from conflict that are redemptive rather than destructive. Instead of simply expecting only hurt to arise out of conflict, I began to pray for and anticipate positive outcomes.

Fourth, I began to exercise my redemptive conflict muscles. Sometimes this has meant rehearsing my words and approach to a conflict situation in order to build confidence. It has also meant going back to an issue that I should have addressed but didn't. In all of this, I have had to readjust my acute sensitivity level related to conflict. Practically, this means recognizing that when I feel like I've been confrontational with someone, it's very unlikely that I've been offensive or overbearing. In fact, I've likely made them just slightly aware that I feel something needs to be addressed.

Fifth, I shared this struggle with some key supporters in my life who are able to encourage, pray and challenge me as needed. They have my permission and my expectation that they will press me or push me when they sense me sliding in this area.

Following the pattern from *Immunity to Change*, I also outlined some signs of significant progress to help me both look forward and evaluate my growth. So, for example, I know if I am moving forward if I am able to share my primary concerns clearly and fully in challenging conversations. Another sign of significant progress is when I have been present in a conflict situation as today's Steve (not eleven-year-old Steve). I have also listed "I am proactive rather than reactive in engaging conflict" as another sign of progress.

In hindsight, I could have spent years learning about conflict styles and skills or trying harder. These things may have helped, but they wouldn't have led to a long-term breakthrough. I needed to get to my competing commitment and address the assumptions underneath. By doing so, I have been able to make new commitments and take positive steps forward. I still wouldn't say I am eager for conflict, but I sense that I now have a much healthier perspective as well as a more biblical response. I am also much quicker to identify when I default back to my old ways.

As you seek to lead yourself and make changes in your life, you will need to take some very practical steps related to knowledge and skills. If you are seeking to get into better shape, you will likely benefit from learning more about nutrition and exercise. If you are seeking to grow in the area of sexual purity and desire to overcome a struggle with pornography, you would likely benefit from adding a software protection program to your computer, tablet and smartphone. If you are seeking to be more contagious in sharing your faith, you need to understand the gospel and how to share it clearly. These kinds of practical steps related to knowledge and skills are very important.

However, don't stop here. Doing so may be like running the lawnmower over dandelions. You may be facing a deeper change, which requires you to get to the roots. This means identifying competing commitments and exploring your assumptions.

Questions can be a great tool in this process. For instance, ask, "What am I believing or doing that is working against my objective?" Then ask, "Why do I believe this? Why am I really doing this or acting in this way? What assumptions are underlying my beliefs and actions?" Another great question may be a prayer where you ask the Lord to reveal if there is a deeper issue keeping you stuck in your old pattern or negative behavior.

Keep probing for the root reasons. You will likely know you are at the root when acting differently seems impossible, highly undesirable or at least difficult. That's your immunity to change fighting back. You've found the roots when it seems too hard to change and far easier to stay with the status quo. When you get here, please remember that the Holy Spirit can override what seems impossible. As Paul wrote in Philippians 4:13, "I can do all this through him who gives me strength."

Identifying competing commitments and addressing assumptions can begin a breakthrough when you start the process of addressing the core issues. Sometimes this will require repentance from false beliefs or behaviors used to meet legitimate needs in illegitimate ways. Sometimes this will require practical and very simple solutions. Sometimes this will require counseling or support from others to address deeper issues over a longer period of time.

Regardless of what is required, as you take forward steps depending on God and a community of support, getting to the roots will free you to move forward. It will also prevent the frustration and eventual despair that sets in when you think trying harder is the only right answer.

Reflection Questions

1. What's an area in your life (present or past) where you've wanted to grow or change but felt stuck or made little progress?

2. Can you identify any competing commitments that have slowed or prevented positive change for you?

3. Following up on question 2, take some time to explore and identify the assumptions underlying the competing commitments that act like antibodies to support the status quo.

4. Following up on question 3, what is a new commitment that you can make to move forward? What would some initial signs of progress look like? What would success look like?

Chapter 12

Key Practice #8
Finding Traction Through Training

What's that noise?! I had been enjoying a deep sleep until the high-pitched whine outside woke me up. Initially I tried to ignore and fight the noise. But after twenty minutes I couldn't take it any longer. I crawled out from underneath the warm blankets and took a quick peek through the blinds to find the source.

It was snowing, and a pickup truck was trying to make it up the icy hill outside our house. The truck would make it three-quarters of the way up. Then it would slowly lose traction. The tires would start spinning, the engine would start whining and the truck wouldn't go another inch forward. At this point, the driver would shift into reverse, back down the hill and make another more determined attempt. The result was the same—over and over.

After briefly considering getting dressed and braving the winter elements to help out, I decided to go back to bed. I could hear the driver make several more unsuccessful attempts. Finally, I heard him back down the hill, and all was quiet.

My hope was that he had given up. I'm not sure whether I was motivated by guilt or compassion, but I got up and peeked through the blinds again. At first I didn't see or hear anything. Then, I saw the headlights and heard the engine roaring again. He was making another attempt. But this time was different.

He passed our house! When he did, I noticed that something was different. The box of the pickup was completely filled with snow. The driver had shoveled the heavy wet snow into the back. The snow's weight on the back axle added just enough traction for the truck to make it to the top of the hill. Finally, he was on his way, and I was heading back to sleep.

I share this illustration because leading yourself can feel a lot like trying to drive your way up an icy hill. We can have a compelling destination in mind for our lives. We can also have a deep reserve of determination to see us get there. But the actual road is often slippery and difficult. Traction becomes a very real problem.

There are many studies and statistics that demonstrate how difficult it is to get traction on forward progress and lasting change in our lives. Many of us try New Year's resolutions. We have good intentions to start a new year with new habits and healthy routines. But most of these well-intentioned resolutions don't get much traction. In fact, twenty-five percent of people abandon their New Year's resolutions after just one week. Sixty percent give up within six months.[1]

Just like the pickup truck driver outside my home, we respond by trying again. Studies show that the average person makes the same New Year's resolution ten separate times without success. We can anticipate that there is growing frustration and even despair in those ten attempts.

Looking at dieting and losing weight, you would think all the diet plans, exercise contraptions, vitamins and gyms would provide amazing traction. Unfortunately, this isn't the case. In reality, 95 percent of those who lose weight on a diet regain it, and a significant percentage gain back more than they originally lost.[2]

One of the most surprising examples of lack of traction is heart attack patients. You would assume that, having had a major health event, heart attack patients would have great inner motivation to do anything and everything to protect their health. After all, their very lives are at stake. In *Change or Die*, Alan Deutschman refers to a study of 37,000 patients with severe heart disease who were prescribed five different popular medicine brands by their doctors. Nearly everyone took their pills for the first month or two, but within three months around half had stopped. By one year later, only one-fifth to one-third were still taking their prescribed medication.[3]

These examples illustrate that it isn't easy to get traction—even when we want to and even when the destination is profoundly important. The trend is to get started but to lose momentum, then to lose traction and then to give up.

For Christ-followers, there is a clear starting place for traction. The starting place is King David's prayer from the book of Psalms (see chapter 2). If this book has inspired a desire in you to grow in a specific area of your life, please remember that traction starts with humility, dependence and trust in God. Whether you desire depth in your intimacy with God, greater holiness, vibrant relationships or to make a profound difference through service, the starting place is humility, dependence and trust.

A posture of humility, dependence and trust brings freedom rather than a burden you cannot bear. You are choosing to walk with the ultimate change agent. You are inviting and depending on the all-powerful Holy Spirit rather than trusting in your own limitations.

From this foundational starting place, 1 Timothy 4:7–8 provides a framework for gaining traction. In this passage Paul admonishes Timothy to "train yourself to be godly. For physical training is of some value, but godliness has value for all things, holding promise for both the present life and the life to come." Let's take a look at each of the three key concepts behind this passage.

1. Training—The first key concept is training. The word "training" rouses images of athletes diligently preparing for their sport. They are in the gym doing reps or on the field practicing. To maximize their training time and effort, most athletes have a specially designed and personalized plan. They don't wing it or idly sit back and just hope for the best. Their training provides an intentional and systematic pathway toward their goals. Their training helps them find traction.

2. Yourself—The second key concept revolves around the word "yourself." If you train yourself, there is an assumption that you are not passive. Instead, you are taking primary responsibility in your training. This means that you need to play a very active role and make clear contributions. You need to take initiative and take action.

As you take responsibility, however, it's key to remember that you are in partnerships. The first partnership is with God. As you "continue to work out your salvation with fear and trembling" (Philippians 2:12), you do so knowing that "it is God who works in you to will and to act in order to fulfill his good purpose" (Philippians 2:13). You are not alone. God is at work in you and through you.

The second partnership is with a community of support. You can't get traction in your own life on our own. You need to invite a community of support to come alongside. As Proverbs 27:17 states, "As iron sharpens iron, so one person sharpens another." You need a community that will practice the "one another" commands from the New Testament. This is a community of those who will love, encourage, accept, bear with, serve, forgive, admonish, provide hospitality, carry your burdens, hear your confessions, speak truth, support you and much more.

In *Change or Die*, Alan Deutschman argues that a community of support is critical for getting traction on change. To support change, he writes, you need to "form a new, emotional relationship with a person or community that inspires and sustains hope." This person or community helps you believe, expect, learn, practice and master change.[4]

My own training regime as a hobby runner illustrates this point. As a runner, I know that I'm much more likely to run if I make a date to run with someone else. This kind of accountability makes a big difference. I also know that I'm much more likely to run farther and faster when I run with others. When I feel like quitting, I'm spurred on by either my running partners or my desire to not fall behind. Either way, I'm encouraged to keep going. It's also usually a lot more fun to tackle a run or race with others.

Practically, I have had to work at inviting others alongside as I train myself to be godly. To do this, I've invited mentors, coaches, pastors, small groups, a spiritual director and peers to help me get traction on leading myself. Without their support and accountability, I'd be like the truck spinning its wheels up the hill.

3. Godliness—Getting back to 1 Timothy 4:7, the third concept that emerges is the goal of training yourself in godliness. The point is transformation into Christlikeness. This takes us back to the big picture of the life of Christ and the four key dimensions of spiritual intimacy, godly character, vibrant relationships and effective service. Growing in Christlikeness is about growing in these four key areas.

A natural question flows from 1 Timothy 4:7 and these three concepts. The question is, how? How do you intentionally train yourself to be godly? Since the early days of the Arrow Leadership Program, there has been an emphasis on empowering Christian leaders to take ownership for their intentional development. The core tool is a highly personalized training plan. For the purposes of this book, I'll call this tool a Leading Me Plan.

A Leading Me Plan is a simple format you can use to intentionally take ownership for your own personal growth. In simple terms, you clearly identify specific objectives for your development. Once these objectives are clearly defined, you create a specific plan to get traction in these areas. (You can find more guidelines and download a blank Leading Me Plan template at www.leadingmebook.com.)

You are the author and owner, so your plan focuses on getting traction on the objectives that you discern are God's priorities for your development. You can invite input from others, but you ultimately determine your priorities and create your plan.

You can also modify your plan anytime to reflect your progress or changes in life. This can include adding a new objective when you sense you have completed or at least have good traction on a current objective. In fact, I would encourage you to update your plan monthly.

A Leading Me Plan has eight key elements:

1. **An Objective Statement**—Your plan flows from a concise and specific objective statement. This is a sentence or two describing how you are seeking to grow and develop. In other words, this statement summarizes your goal and desired outcome.

    For example, this is an objective on physical health (which would flow from the character gauge): e(Why)

    > I want to better steward my physical health, increase my energy level and improve my fitness so I can be more focused at work and have energy left at the end of the day for my family.

2. **Future Vision**—Once you have identified your one or two objectives, the next step is to outline what success looks like. This means painting a positive and inspiring word picture of what your future reality will be like if and when you get traction on your objective.

    This word picture (or if you are more artistic, you can draw or paint a real picture) describes what the future would be like with this change. This picture should inspire you. It's something you can go back to for encouragement when things are hard. When you are wondering if the training is worth the effort, this picture will tell you it is!

145

Research demonstrates that we are pulled *toward* a positive outcome. So, for this section, list the compelling positive reasons for this change. Put things into the positive. Instead of describing all the things you won't do or don't want to do, reframe to the positive. For example, this might be your positive envisioned future statement:

> Long-term, I'm at my kid's college graduation and in good health. Medium-term, I have more than enough energy to play with my kids and navigate daily life. I can play sports with vigor again. I'm back at my healthy body weight. I'm free from my caffeine and sugar habits and have self-control when I shop for food and eat.

3. **Inspiring Verse**—Is there a Bible verse that brings energy, focus and inspiration to your objective statement? Grounding your objective in God's Word adds another dimension. This is about not just your desires but also God's desires and plans for your life.

   As an example, your inspiring verse for the objective to better steward your physical health might be 2 Timothy 2:21. Personalized, it reads, "I desire to be an 'instrument for special purposes, made holy, useful to the Master and prepared to do any good work.'"

4. **Current Reality**—One of the most important roles for a leader is to discern and define reality. Knowing where you are is incredibly important. This component of your Leading Me Plan asks you to define your current reality in this area. Though it may be hard, it's important to be brutally honest. The purpose isn't to add guilt or load you down with discouragement. The purpose is to provide a clear starting point that you can look back on down the road. It's also an invitation for God's help as he joins you in your training.

   For our sample objective on stewarding physical health, this might be the current reality:

> My doctor lectures me about my health and weight (I'm 50 pounds over my ideal weight). I get winded going up flights of stairs. I have little energy and can't exist without lots of coffee. I rely on food to comfort me, and my eating sometimes gets out of control. My spouse is concerned and unhappy about my self-care, and my kids make jokes about my body.

5. **Competing Commitments**—Your discipline and the intentionality of your plan will help you move forward on your objectives. However,

as already addressed in the chapter on dealing with dandelions, it's essential to seek out and identify the beliefs or behaviors that you engage in or don't engage in that work against desired change.

Unless you identify and address these competing commitments you won't get to the assumptions that are holding you back from traction on your objective. Instead, these assumptions will be protecting the status quo. Look for the root causes in answering these questions: What are you are believing, doing or not doing to reinforce your current behavior? What are the assumptions underlying these beliefs and behaviors?

For our example, these might be two competing commitments:

1. Work is a stressful environment, and I feel entitled and comforted by eating foods that I know are bad for me.

2. I commute 90 minutes daily, so I don't have time or energy at the end of the day to exercise.

Once you have identified your competing commitments and the underlying values, you can address them in your action plan.

6. Action Plan and Timeline—You have established your objectives, and you have an inspiring picture of the future with traction on these objectives. You have honestly laid out your current reality, and you have identified your competing commitments. The next step is to develop an action plan and timeline.

Your action plan lays out specific action steps that will help you achieve your objective. Some of these action steps will be one-time steps, and some will be regular new rhythms that you hope to establish.

One-time steps are actions that have a clear beginning and ending. They are not open-ended or ongoing. At some point, you can check them off as complete. For the example objective, these might be some one-time steps:

• One-Time: Go to doctor for a physical (by end of year)

• One-Time: Read one book on healthy eating (in next three months)

Be sure to add when each step will be completed or started in brackets beside the step. Remember to consider other responsibilities you have and that taking steps forward often take longer than we think!

Ongoing rhythms are just that—ongoing practices that you are seeking to incorporate in your life for a season or even for the long haul. You can't check them off as finished. These rhythms may be of varying frequency—daily, weekly, monthly, quarterly, yearly, etc.

In his award-winning book *God in My Everything*, Ken Shigematsu encourages Christ-followers to adopt a pattern of rhythms in their lives. These rhythms work together to form what has been called a "rule of life." The idea of a rule of life comes from the Greek word that means "trellis." Shigematsu writes,

> A trellis is a support system for a vine or plant that enables it to grow upward and bear fruit. For a grapevine to produce good grapes it must have a trellis to support and guide its growth or it will slump to the ground. When this happens the fruit tends to rot before it ripens.[5]

The practice of these rhythms and this rule keeps Christ in the center of our lives and gives support to living these practices out in our every day. For this example, a new rhythm could be getting to the gym and working out three times per week.

As you identify your action steps, it is also important to remember to start small. This should be intuitive, but most of us are tempted to think big too quickly. If your objective is to better steward your physical health, you could be tempted to jump right in by pledging to wake up at 5 a.m. every day to run five miles before breakfast. However, if your current reality is that you get winded going up several flights of stairs and you haven't run five miles in fifteen years, you are most likely setting yourself up for failure.

Instead, you should start small and build on small successes. Change specialist John Kotter writes that organizations and individuals making changes need "victories that nourish faith in the change effort, emotionally reward the hard workers, keep the critics at bay, and build momentum."[6] This means that you should plan action steps that are a stretch but doable. When you achieve that action step, celebrate it and use your success as traction to keep moving forward.

7. Resources Needed—What resources are needed for you to implement your action plan? For example, do you need books, courses, time, a coach, a counselor, a gym membership, etc.? Also, reflect on

the people and community support you need. Whose support do you need to invite? Make a practical list in this section.

Following our example, these might be your resources for stewarding your physical health:

- Doctor's appointment for physical
- Book on healthy eating
- Gym membership for working out
- Accountability from two friends

8. **Review**—Your Leading Me Plan is almost complete. This step ensures that you will intentionally review your progress and level of traction. The adage "you can expect what you inspect" is an important encouragement to be intentional about taking time to evaluate. Specifically, you need to determine the following:

- Where will you keep your plan?
- How often and when will you review your plan?
- How will you evaluate your progress?
- What adjustments and modifications need to be made?

Keeping your plan where you can see it is important. Your Leading Me Plan should be a simple and relatively brief document that inspires you. So find a place to put it or post it as a reminder and encourager. For instance, you could put your plan in your journal or post it someplace where you can see it.

As to how often and when you review your plan, I would encourage a weekly review. Your review doesn't need to take a lot of time, but a weekly rhythm will help keep you focused. Ideally, you should seek a fifteen-minute window at the same time every week.

Self-evaluation questions can be a great tool for your review. These are questions you can just ask yourself. They are related to your action steps but need to be grounded in the desired outcomes expressed in your objective. Using our example, two self-evaluation questions might be the following:

1. On a scale of 1 to 10, how is my energy?
2. On a scale of 1 to 10, how much traction am I getting on new eating habits and a rhythm of exercise?

You can answer these two questions pretty quickly. If you track your weekly answers in a journal or notebook, you will begin to see trends. You can also just update the "Current Reality" section on your Leading Me Plan. As you do this over time, hopefully you will begin to see a trend of traction toward your objective.

The next step is to ask what adjustments and modifications need to be made. This is an important reminder that your Leading Me Plan isn't static. It can be and should be changing regularly. For instance, if you complete a one-time action step, you can mark it "complete" or even delete it from your plan. You should pause to celebrate!

You may also discover that part of your plan isn't working. Maybe there has been a new development in your life that reduces the amount of time you have to invest in your objective. If this is the case, you can reduce the intensity or the timelines for your action steps. It is better to take this step and be realistic than to be discouraged because you are continually falling behind.

The same advice goes for any part of your plan where you have experienced significant traction. First, you should celebrate your progress. Second, ask whether you should modify the intensity or timeline of your action steps to add more challenge.

Remember, the leadership plan is designed to serve you, not for you to serve it! It should be a simple document. Using our downloadable template, it should be one to three pages maximum. Something has gotten off track if it has become complicated or burdensome.

To give some broader perspective on your expectations for traction, it is important to step back for a moment. As you look at your objectives, please recognize that all change initiatives are not equal.

You have likely heard the rule of thumb that forming a habit requires repetition of the desired behavior for forty days. This isn't true. According to Tony Schwartz in *The Way We're Working Isn't Working*, the speed of change depends on a number of factors.[7] For starters, it depends on our level of motivation to change. How badly do we want to change? What level of energy and attention are we willing to invest in the change?

The speed of change also depends on the complexity of the new behaviors. For example, if I am seeking to be a brain surgeon, I will need more than forty days to learn the complex new behaviors required. Similarly, someone who has been living on the streets for years will likely need significant time to adjust to living in his or her own home.

Our frequency of practice is another factor. For instance, if you are trying to grow as a public speaker, more speaking opportunities will usually speed up your growth.

In summary, a Leading Me Plan can be a powerful tool to help you gain traction as you seek to lead yourself intentionally. It allows you to take initiative and responsibility for your own growth and development. It clearly positions you to partner with God and others. And it provides a pathway to take clear action steps and develop ongoing rhythms in your life and leadership.

Reflection Questions

1. How has getting traction for change and growth been challenging to you?

2. When you reflect on 1 Timothy 4:7 in the context of a partnership between God, you and a community of support, what questions, encouragement or challenges come to mind?

3. As you reflect on Leading Me and your life, what area of your development would you like to gain traction in?

4. What are your next steps to get traction?

Chapter 13

Running with Perseverance

By all indications Mark seemed to have "arrived." He was a successful CEO in his early sixties, leading at the top of his game. Mark helped to found the organization several decades back. From its start with a big idea, a few committed staff and limited funds, the organization experienced significant growth over next couple of decades. Fast forward past lots of hard and prayerful work to the present, and they are an industry leader with thousands of clients and hundreds of staff managing several billions of dollars in assets.

As Mark was sharing his inspiring story with a class of the Arrow Leadership Program, it seemed like he could choose to simply coast into retirement. Then Mark made this declaration: "Who you are today isn't fit to lead your organization five years from now." In other words, if you personally don't keep learning, growing and developing, then it won't be very long until you won't be effective as a team or an organizational leader. Mark went on to share that he wasn't coasting. He was continuing to make his own personal leadership a top priority by regularly taking courses at top schools, investing significant time in reading, learning everything he can from people around him at all levels of his organization and being stretched through regular executive coaching.

Mark's statement was sobering. I sometimes dream that I will "arrive." I imagine a day when I wake up and magically won't need to do the hard work of leading myself. But Mark's words and example are a clear reminder that there's no arriving in this life. A more senior title and position doesn't mark our arrival. In fact, just the opposite is true. The more responsibility we have for leading others and leading organizations, the more intentional personal leadership is required.

When I think about Mark's example, I remember the words of Paul Stanley. Paul served for several decades internationally in senior roles with the Navigators, and he shared this adage with Arrow classes over the years: "Peak at eighty." In other words, keep intentionally growing, learning, contributing and leading so that you hit the height of your effectiveness when you are eighty.

Mark's words also bring me back to these rich words found in Hebrews 12:1–3:

> Therefore, since we are surrounded by such a great cloud of witnesses, let us throw off everything that hinders and the sin that so easily entangles. And let us run with perseverance the race marked out for us, fixing our eyes on Jesus, the pioneer and perfecter of faith. For the joy set before him he endured the cross, scorning its shame, and sat down at the right hand of the throne of God. Consider him who endured such opposition from sinners, so that you will not grow weary and lose heart.

As a fairly avid runner, I can relate to the challenge to "run with perseverance the race marked out for us." I know what it's like to wake up early on a cold, dark and wet morning to train. I've had to fight the temptation to sleep in or put it off for another day. I've stood in the starting corral for large races where you are packed tight with hundreds or even thousands of other runners. There's a buzz of excitement combined with some uncertainty about the course ahead and how your body will respond.

In these races I've had easy miles and hard ones. Stunning scenery, the encouragement of race-day spectators and learning the inspiring stories of fellow runners have made for many easy miles. On the flipside, I've battled up hills that seem relentless and endless. I've also endured rain and heat, fought boredom and loneliness, overcome blisters and fatigue, and pressed through my biggest challenge—my own negative thinking, which quickly leads to weariness and ultimately losing heart.

Though you may not be able to relate to long-distance running, you and I are running a race. It's a race unique to each of us. We don't fully know the distance. For some it will be longer, and for others it will be shorter. Though there may be some easy miles, we are promised that the race will not be easy. Yet this race has been marked out for you and for me—and we are called to run with perseverance to the finish.

Running your race with perseverance may include many leadership assignments and challenges. For a few, the race will include the call to wisely lead an organization, or at least part of one. For some, the race will involve effectively leading others. However, for everyone the race will require personal leadership in partnership with God.

You are your most important leadership assignment. You are also often your most difficult one. My prayer is that *Leading Me* has helped you capture God's big-picture intention and desire for you to live a life of deep spiritual intimacy, godly and healthy character, vibrant relationships in community and significant service for God's glory.

I also pray that the eight practices will give you a practical framework for leading yourself as you run the race marked out for you. To recap, here are the eight key practices with connection to Hebrews 12:1–3 and the metaphor of a race:

Key Practice #1—Growing Your Vision—In a race, it's easy to keep your eyes on many things. There are other runners, some who run with ease and others who move slowly. It's also tempting to focus on the scenery or the hills ahead or your own discomfort. The passage in Hebrews calls us to fix "our eyes on Jesus, the pioneer and perfecter of faith" (Hebrews 12:2). This call is rooted in the reality that your vision of God is central to how you think and how you act. Growing your vision means to cultivate a bigger, clearer and fuller vision of God. Central to this bigger vision of God is really knowing and internalizing the magnitude of his great love.

Key Practice #2—Identifying Bungees—Hebrews 12:1 tells us to "throw off everything that hinders and the sin that so easily entangles." Races are hard enough to run without hindrances or bungee cords. Identifying bungees means discerning whatever is holding you back and throwing off all that hinders and the sin that so easily entangles.

Key Practice #3—Keeping Connected—Most running races include many lonely miles sandwiched between crowds at the beginning and the end. The list of faithful saints and servants in Hebrews 11 is a vivid reminder that there is a great cloud of witnesses sending you off and meeting you at the end of your race. Though you will run many miles on your own, this practice is about being intentional in nurturing a constellation of vibrant relationships that form a strong community around you.

Key Practice #4—Taking Care of Me—Your physical health is key to running any race. To lead yourself well means maximizing your energy and health through stewardship of your most important asset—you. In practical terms this means developing habits and rhythms to ensure proper sleep, healthy nutrition and regular exercise, as well as rest and renewal.

Key Practice #5—Leveraging Your Impact—The race marked out for you is significant. It's significant because God has marked it out for you. It's also significant because you have just this one race to run. Leveraging your impact calls you to intentionally steward the direction and gifts God has already given to you in a way that maximizes your impact and shalom.

Key Practice #6—Managing Your Time—Runners usually run with an eye on the time. Running at too fast a pace early on often leads to reduced energy or worse as you add on miles. Running too slowly leads to not maximizing your training and a slower time at the finish. Managing your time is about taking practical steps and using proven tools to be a faithful steward and experience shalom.

Key Practice #7—Dealing with Dandelions—Too often we seek to initiate change or tackle struggles without addressing the root issues below the surface. Our quick-fix solution may bring some initial positive change, but before long the same old behaviors appear and greater frustration sets in. Dealing with your dandelions is about getting to the roots—the things that hinder—and dealing with them in order to establish new healthy patterns.

Key Practice #8—Finding Traction Through Training—Seeking to run a race without training is not only unwise, it's foolish. This practice seeks to help you take responsibility for your training, develop a clear training plan and address major issues that undermine your traction.

As you seek to continue run your race with perseverance, be encouraged! We can be confident of this: "that he who began a good work in you will carry it on to completion until the day of Christ Jesus" (Philippians 1:6).

See you at the finish!

Acknowledgements

Inever anticipated ever writing a book. In fact, I was opposed to doing so for a number of reasons. Then, one day during a solo retreat three years ago, a rough outline came to me in the course of an afternoon. I knew then that I needed to get over my reluctance and get writing.

My writing journey has been slower, faster, harder and easier than I thought. As with most things, the most difficult challenge has been leading myself in the midst of regularly scheduled life and the demands of leadership. But the journey of this book has been richer and better because of the encouragement, support and help of so many.

To the following group and many others I owe my deepest thanks:

Thank you, Lea, for being my best friend, co-adventurer in life and an amazing mom. Luke, Ainslea and Lauren, thank you for your love, grace, and patience. Thank you for the gift of time to write and for putting life into perspective.

I'm especially grateful for Brenda Pue's valuable feedback and detailed review of the first draft. This was a special gift from a wise mentor, esteemed colleague and trusted friend.

Leading Me is stronger and sharper thanks to the editorial insights of Jody Cross, Darren DeGraaf, Julian Dunham, Rick Franklin, James Lawrence, Mitchel Lee, Carl Nash, and Jennifer Parr. Beyond this book, I also know that I'm much stronger and sharper thanks to each of you!

There have been many mentors and encouragers along the road of my life. Thank you, Dad, for the gift of time and for the best business training on the water and the back porch. Thank you, Lisa, for watching out for your little brother and for ongoing encouragement.

Josh and Dottie McDowell, Dave and Linette Boyes, Bill and Peggy Fitch, John Wilkinson, Miller Alloway, Paul and Christa Schoeber,

Bobb Biehl, John McAuley, Wayne Johnson, Keith Anderson, Mark Buchanan, Evon Hedley, Steve Imbach, Doug Alexander, Mark Peterkins, Peter Roebbelen, Curt Erb, Ken Shigematsu and Chris Wignall: you have been amazing examples, friends, mentors and encouragers. Thank you!

Steve and Evy Klassen and the team at The Mark Centre have provided for over ten years a safe oasis for me to regularly slow down, pray, listen and think. Much of this book was written in this special space. Thank you, too, Mountain Park Community Church for welcoming the Brown family and for faithfully seeking Matthew 6:33.

This book wouldn't be a book without the capable and experienced guidance of Larry Willard, Marina Hofman Willard, the Castle Quay Books team and the support of Stronger Together 2013. Thank you for your vision to grow leaders!

I love being part of the Arrow community. Ironically, I almost didn't make it through my first residential session back in 2000. I've been thankful for Carson Pue's encouragement ever since. Special thanks to Tarra Wellings, for faithfully serving alongside me for over a decade with grace, perseverance and much wisdom, as well as our faithful team of Gretchen Englund, Doug Ward, Mitch Whitman, Taylor Williams, Denise Ellis, Alison Boettcher, Michelle Tydeman and so many dedicated volunteers and generous supporters. It's a joy and privilege to serve with you. Your relentless service to God and Christian leaders is so important and so not in vain.

Finally, I'm thankful to the hundreds of Arrow leaders who have given the gift of trust by inviting me in and allowing me to walk alongside them as part of God's polishing process in their lives. May each of us continue to be "led more by Jesus, lead more like Jesus and lead more to Jesus."

Steps to Crafting a Personal Vision Statement

Step 1: Taking Inventory

Set aside some time to reflect on your SHAPE (see Rick Warren/Saddleback Church for more):

- **SPIRITUAL GIFTS**—What are your spiritual gifts? How have these been evidenced and affirmed by the body of Christ? Take a spiritual gift inventory if you haven't already.

- **HEART**—What do you love to do? What passions, activities and interests bring you life? Do you have a "holy discontent" about a certain issue? Conversely, what drains you?

- **ABILITIES**—What are your greatest strengths? Take the StrengthsFinder inventory or ask the people around you for input.

- **PERSONALITY**—What do you know about your personality? List some important realities in point form. Take the MBTI or other personality inventories to learn more.

- **EXPERIENCE**—Reflect on your life to date—how has your family, education, vocation, spiritual journey, friends, mentors, and painful times shaped you to be who you are? What have been five to ten key life turning points for you?

  Spend some time prayerfully reflecting. Do any trends or themes begin to emerge in how God has been shaping you? If so, spend some time considering how might this inform or impact the particular vision God has for your life and leadership.

Step 2: Probing Outside the Box

While discerning God's vision for your life is something you cannot manufacture or control the timing of, you may be able to discover some hints or affirm what he has already made clear (which may be more than you think).

Spend a significant block of time (a morning, afternoon or evening) in prayerful solitude to journal and reflect on one or all of the following:

- Write the speech (narrative with sentences or point form) you would like to have shared at your retirement party. Write with a holistic focus and include what you would want your colleagues and friends to say about the four key dimensions of your life:
  1. **Spiritual Intimacy**—What would you want highlighted about your personal connection and relationship with God?
  2. **Character**—What would you want remembered about your character?
  3. **Relationships**—What would you want people to notice about how you prioritized and connected with your family, friends, church, people on their way to God, the poor and marginalized, etc.?
  4. **Service**—How would you want your impact and legacy to be recorded?

- *In Holy Discontent*, Bill Hybels writes that God often inspires a deep discontent within a leader about a problem or situation. Like with Nehemiah's deep anguish over the news about Jerusalem, from the discontent God can stir a particular calling in the life of a leader. Do you have a "holy discontent" about an issue, situation or problem? What is it? Why does this stir you? What do you desire to do about it?

- If you were guaranteed it was part of God's will, your friends would support you, you had all the resources required and it would succeed, what three things would you most like to do for God's glory over the next five years?

Step 3: Synergy—Begin to Write What You Do Know

Exercise 1

- Pray, asking God to continue to reveal more of his direction and to guide you as you seek to discover synergy between your work in steps 1 and 2.

- Review and overlay your work in steps 1 and 2. Does anything "percolate"? Do you sense or see or hear the start of synergy in what God has and is and will do in your life? Write it down.

Exercise 2

- Start in point form or sentences, whichever is your preference, and write a first draft of what you know so far (or at least think you know) about God's vision for your life. Again, write from a holistic perspective (remember—God cares about your entire life and not just your output over the next few decades), and once again, use the four headings—spiritual intimacy, godly character, community/relationships and service—as a framework.

• Don't worry about trying to "wordsmith" (get every word perfect) in this exercise. Know, too, that it may take a couple of sittings to write this draft, so give yourself some breaks (which may prompt some missing pieces in your mind).

• Also, don't worry about length—you aren't trying to fit this on a T-shirt or bumper sticker or business card. Be free to write and write.

Step 4: Sharpen, Test and Refine

Let your work from step 3 "simmer" and settle for a little while. Don't rush forward.

Exercise 1

Prayerfully review your work from step 3. You will likely spot some missing pieces, some areas that could be tightened up to be more succinct and some areas that need some "wordsmithing" to more clearly articulate what you are trying to capture. At this stage, spend some time adding, tightening and wordsmithing. Invite a friend gifted in writing to help if you desire.

Exercise 2

Go back over your vision statement and try to distill it down to 120 words.

Exercise 3

When you read over your personal vision statement, you can evaluate it with these questions:

• **Surrender**—Am I willing to follow my Master?

• **Personal**—Is this unique to me?

• **Purpose**—Is it compelling?

• **Passion**—Does reading it fill me with energy?

• **Priorities**—Does it help me say "yes" and "no"?

• **Prayerfulness**—Does seeking to live it out put me on my knees?

- **Perseverance**—Will it motivate me to press on in the midst of challenges and obstacles?

- **Community**—Do those that know me best and the community of God's people affirm my vision statement?

Exercise 4

Invite input from some godly advisors. Sharpen and rework as necessary. But be careful to stay true to the core areas that God is calling you to.

Step 5: Gap Analysis

If you believe you have discerned some of God's call for your life, you need to respond with obedience as a faithful steward. This means regularly identifying the gaps between God's desire and your reality and then making, in his power, steps to get back or more on track.

Exercise 1

By design, a vision calls us from where we are to a more preferable place and state. This movement requires evaluation, planning and change. The following questions are designed to help stimulate regular evaluation (monthly or quarterly is suggested) and focus planning to allow change.

- Review your personal vision statement in sections—spiritual intimacy, character, relationships and service. For each, ask,

  1. Is there growing health and momentum in this area?

  2. If yes, what is helping to promote health and momentum?

  3. If no, what are the hindrances? Is there a root issue behind what may be symptoms? How can this be addressed?

  4. What needs to change to see more health, growth and momentum toward God's desire? How can you make a manageable and reasonable plan to move forward?

Endnotes

Introduction

[1] Robert Clinton, *The Making of a Leader* (Colorado Springs: NavPress, 1988), 31.

[2] Dee Hock, "The Art of Chaordic Leadership," *Leader to Leader*, Leader to Leader Institute and Jossey-Bass, 2000.

Chapter 1

[1] Henry Cloud and John Townsend, *How People Grow* (Grand Rapids: Zondervan, 2001), 67.

[2] Cloud and Townsend, *How People Grow*, 69.

[3] Ken Shigematsu, *God in My Everything* (Grand Rapids: Zondervan, 2013), 23.

[4] Jim Collins, "Level 5 Leadership—The Triumph of Humility and Fierce Resolve," *Harvard Business Review* (July–August 2005): 7.

Chapter 2

[1] Leighton Ford, *Transforming Leadership* (Downer's Grove: InterVarsity Press, 1993), 38.

[2] Os Guinness, *The Call* (Nashville: Thomas Nelson, 2003), 31.

[3] George Barna, *A Fish out of Water* (Nashville: Thomas Nelson, 2002), 95.

[4] Andy Stanley, *Next Generation Leader* (Colorado Springs: Multnomah, 2006), 151.

[5] Stanley, *Next Generation Leader*, 131.

[6] Dallas Willard, *Renovation of the Heart* (Colorado Springs: NavPress, 2002), 182.

[7] James Lawrence, *Growing Leaders* (Oxfordshire: The Bible Reading Fellowship, 2004), 128.

[8] Lawrence, *Growing Leaders*, 33.

[9] Frank E. Gaebelein, ed., *The Expositor's Bible Commentary, Vol. 1* (Grand Rapids: Zondervan, 1979), 416.

Chapter 3

[1] Joy Milos, "Evelyn Underhill: a companion on many journeys" in *Traditions of Spiritual Guidance*, ed. Lavinia Byrne (Geoffrey Chapman 1990), 138.

[2] A. W. Tozer, *The Knowledge of the Holy* (New York: HarperOne, 1978), 9.

[3] James Lawrence adapted the model from the Christian psychiatrist Frank Lake's study of John's Gospel and suggestion that in Jesus' life there was a rhythm of ongoing input that led to appropriate output.

[4] James Lawrence, *Growing Leaders*.

[5] Bill Hybels, *Courageous Leadership* (Grand Rapids: Zondervan, 2008), 216–7.

[6] Henry Cloud, *Changes That Heal* (Grand Rapids: Zondervan, 1992), 22.

[7] Cloud, *Changes That Heal*, 23.

[8] Henri Nouwen, *The Return of the Prodigal Son* (New York: Doubleday, 1994).

[9] Matt Redman, "The Father's Song," *The Father's Song*, performed by Matt Redman, Survivor Records, CD, 2000.

[10] Brennan Manning, *Ragamuffin Gospel* (Multnomah Books, 2005), 19.

[11] Henri Nouwen, *In the Name of Jesus* (New York: The Crossroad Publishing Company, 1992), 43.

[12] Tozer, *The Knowledge of the Holy*, 126.

Chapter 4

[1] Carson Pue, *Mentoring Leaders* (Grand Rapids: Baker Books, 2005).

Chapter 5

[1] Dietrich Bonhoeffer, *Life Together* (New York: HarperOne, 2009), 82–83.

[2] Bonhoeffer, *Life Together*, 82–83.

[3] Cloud and Townsend, *How People Grow*, 122.

[4] Hybels, *Courageous Leadership*, 99.

[5] Lawrence, *Growing Leaders*, 98.

[6] Paul D. Stanley and Robert J. Clinton, *Connecting: Mentoring Relationships You Need To Succeed* (Colorado Springs: NavPress, 1992).

Chapter 6

[1] Rick Warren, Daniel Amen and Mark Hymen, *The Daniel Plan* (Grand Rapids: Zondervan, 2013), 13.

[2] Body Mass Index, which is a function of height and weight, is a common tool used to determine if someone is overweight or obese.

[3] Centers for Disease Control and Prevention, "Adult Obesity Facts," accessed September 2014, www.cdc.gov/obesity/data/adult.html.

[4] Karen C. Roberts, Margot Shields, Margaret de Groh, Alfred Aziz and Jo-Anne Gilbert, "Overweight and obesity in children and adolescents: Results from the 2009 to 2011 Canada Health Measures Survey," Statistics Canada, accessed September 2014, http://www.statcan.gc.ca/pub/82–003-x/2012003/article/11706-eng.htm.

[5] Stephen Adams, "Obesity Killing Three Time as Many as Malnutrition," *The Telegraph*, December 13, 2012, http://www.telegraph.co.uk/health/healthnews/9742960/Obesity-killing-three-times-as-many-as-malnutrition.html.

[6] S. N. Blair et al., "Body-Mass Index and Mortality in a Prospective Cohort of U.S. Adults," *The New England Journal of Medicine* 341 (1999): 1097–1105.

[7] Maggie Fox, "Heavyburden: Obesity may be even deadlier than thought," NBC News, August 15, 2013, accessed September 2014, http://www.nbcnews.com/health/health-news/heavy-burden-obesity-may-be-even-deadlier-thought-f6C10930019.

[8] E. A. Finkelstein, J. G. Trogdon, J. W. Cohen, and W. Dietz, "Annual medical spending attributable to obesity: Payer-and service-specific estimates," *Health Affairs* 2009; 28 (5): w822-w831.

[9] Rae Jean Proeschold-Bell and Sara LeGrand, "Physical Health Function Among United Methodist Clergy," *Journal of Religion and Health*, July 2010, accessed September 2014, http://divinity.duke.edu/initiatives-centers/clergy-health-initiative/what-we're-learning/published-research-0.

[10] "Chronic Diseases: The Power to Prevent, The Call to Control," Centers for Disease Control and Prevention, 2009, http://www.cdc.gov/chronicdisease/resources/publications/aag/chronic.htm.

[11] Jim Loehr, *The Power of Story* (New York: Free Press, 2007), 174.

[12] Loehr, *The Power of Story*, 173.

[13] Gary Thomas, *Every Body Matters* (Grand Rapids: Zondervan, 2011) 15.

[14] Dan Buettner, *Blue Zones* (Washington: National Geographic Society, 2012).

[15] Buettner, *Blue Zones*, 124.

[16] Buettner, *Blue Zones*, 128.

[17] Buettner, *Blue Zones*, 129.

[18] Christopher P. Neck, Tedd L. Mitchell, Charles C. Manz, Emmet C. Thompson II, and Janet Tornelli-Mitchell, *Fit To Lead* (Franklin: Carpenter's Son Publishing, 2012), 23.

Chapter 7

[1] Tony Schwartz, *The Way We're Working Isn't Working* (New York: Free Press, 2010), 57.

[2] Luiza Ch. Savage, "Go To Bed. On Time. (Or else.) Sleep crisis: The science of slumber," *Maclean's*, June 17, 2013.

[3] "Insufficient Sleep Is a Public Health Epidemic," Centers for Disease Control and Prevention, accessed September 2014, http://www.cdc.gov/Features/dsSleep/.

[4] *Journal of Occupational and Environmental Medicine*, January 2010; 52 (1): 91–8.

[5] Greg McKeown, *Essentialism* (New York, Crown Publishing Group, 2014), 94.

[6] Cheri Mah, Kenneth Mah, Eric Kezirian, et al., "The effects of sleep extension on the athletic performance of collegiate basketball players," *Sleep* 34, no. 7 (Jul 2011): 943–950. Total objective nightly sleep time increased during sleep extension compared to baseline by 110.9 ± 79.7 min (P < 0.001).

[7] Jim Loehr and Tony Schwartz, *The Power of Full Engagement* (New York: The Free Press, 2003), 61.

[8] Tony Schwartz, "Relax! You'll Be More Productive," *The New York Times*, February 10, 2013: 1.

[9] Loehr and Schwartz, *The Power of Full Engagement*, 61.

[10] "Food Consumption in America: What Are We Eating?" Visual Economics: The Credit Blog, 2010, http://www.creditloan.com/blog/food-consumption-in-america/.

[11] Neck et al., *Fit to Lead*, 23.

[12] Thomas, *Every Body Matters*, 15.

[13] "Sugary Drinks and Obesity Fact Sheet," Harvard School of Public Health, 2013. http://www.hsph.harvard.edu/nutritionsource/sugary-drinks-fact-sheet/.

[14] McDonald's Nutrition Center, accessed September 2014, http://www.mcdonalds.ca/ca/en/food/nutrition_centre.html#/.

[15] Neck et al., *Fit To Lead*, 78.

[16] Jim Loehr and Tony Schwartz, "The Making of a Corporate Athlete," *Harvard Business Review*, January 2001, 124.

[17] Schwartz, *The Way We're Working Isn't Working*, 81.

[18] Neck et al., *Fit To Lead*, 23.

[19] Kathleen Fackelmann, "Author: Regular Workouts 'Spark' Brain," *USA Today*, February 19, 2008, 12D, www.usatoday.com/news/health/2008–02–18-brain-spark_N.htm (January 7, 2011).

[20] Schwartz, "Relax! You'll Be More Productive."

[21] "Vacations A Prescription for Health and Happiness, Expedia.ca's Annual Vacation Deprivation Survey Finds," July 23, 2014, accessed September 2014, http://press.expedia.ca.node/1756.

[22] Schwartz, *The Way We're Working Isn't Working*, 76.

[23] 38% of Canadians survey respondents say they regularly or constantly check work email and/or voicemail while on vacation—up from 27 per cent last year.

[24] Baratunde Thurston, "#Unplug: Baratunde Thurston Left the Internet for 25 Days and You Should Too," *Fast Company*, July/August 2013. "Vacations A Prescription for Health and Happiness, Expedia.ca's Annual Vacation Deprivation Survey Finds," July 23, 2014, accessed September 2014, http://press.expedia.ca.node/1756.

[25] Gordon MacDonald, *Building Below the Waterline* (Peabody: Hendrickson Publishers, 2011), 87.

Chapter 8

[1] Wayne Mueller, *Sabbath: Finding Rest, Renewal and Delight in our Busy Lives* (New York: Bantam Books, 2000, 10.

[2] Mark Buchanan, *The Rest of God* (Nashville: Thomas Nelson, 2007), 61.

Chapter 9

1 Tim Chester, *The Busy Christian's Guide to Busyness* (Nottingham: Inter-Varsity Press, 2006), 48.

2 Andy Stanley, *Visioneering* (Sisters: Multnomah, 1999), 125.

3 Ravi Zacharias, *The Grand Weaver* (Grand Rapids: Zondervan, 2007), 65.

4 Tim Keller, *Every Good Endeavor* (New York: Dutton, 2012), 20.

5 Greg Ogden, *Transformational Discipleship* (Downer's Grove: Inter-Varsity Press, 2003), 69.

6 Phil Vischer, *Me, Myself and Bob* (Nashville: Thomas Nelson, 2006), 251.

7 Ford, *Transforming Leadership*, 104.

8 Guinness, *The Call*, 46.

9 Guinness, *The Call*, 67.

10 Guinness, *The Call*, 133.

Chapter 10

1 Peter Drucker, *The Effective Executive* (New York: HarperCollins Publishers, 2001), 226.

2 Buchanan, *The Rest of God*, 82.

3 MacDonald, *Building Below the Waterline*, 85.

4 MacDonald, *Building Below the Waterline*, 80.

5 Stephen Covey, *First Things First* (New York: Simon and Schuster, 1994), 88–89.

6 You can learn more about Bobb Biehl at www.bobbbiehl.com.

7 Peter Drucker, interview by Bruce Rosenstein, April 11, 2005. Bruce wrote up the interview in his book *Living in More Than One World: How Peter Drucker's Wisdom Can Inspire and Transform Your Life* (San Francisco: Berrett-Koehler, 2009).

8 Bobb Biehl, *Leadership Insights* (Mt. Dora: Aylen Publishing), 22.

9 Faith Brynie, "The Madness of Multitasking," *Psychology Today* (August 24, 2009).

10 Matt Richtel, "Digital Devices Deprive Brain of Needed Downtime," *NY Times*, August 24, 2010.

11 Matt Perman, *What's Best Next* (Grand Rapids: Zondervan, 2014), 242.

Chapter 11

[1] Robert Kegan and Lisa Laskow Lahey, *Immunity to Change* (Boston: Harvard Business School Publishing, 2009), 38.

Chapter 12

[1] Schwartz, *The Way We're Working Isn't Working*, 33.
[2] Schwartz, *The Way We're Working Isn't Working*, 33.
[3] Alan Deutschman, *Change or Die* (New York: HarperCollins Publisher, 2007), 40.
[4] Deutschman, *Change or Die*, 41.
[5] Shigematsu, *God in My Everything*, 21.
[6] John P. Kotter and Dan S. Cohen, *The Heart of Change: Real-Life Stories of How People Change Their Organizations* (Boston: Harvard Business School Press, 2002), 101.
[7] Schwartz, *The Way We're Working Isn't Working*, 38.

About the Author

D r. Steve Brown is husband to Lea and dad to Luke, Ainslea and Lauren. They live in Abbotsford, British Columbia. For over a decade Steve has directed the Arrow Leadership Program in North America, and he now serves as president. Steve has journeyed alongside hundreds of Christian leaders, leveraging his leadership experience serving in local church, denominational, para-church and marketplace roles. A graduate of Wilfrid Laurier University (HBBA), Tyndale Seminary (MDiv) and Gordon-Conwell Theological Seminary (DMin), Steve's goal is to equip leaders to cultivate spiritual vibrancy, develop healthy and holy character, grow deep relationships and leverage their leadership for maximum impact. Steve is also the author of *Great Questions for Leading Well* as well as the primary contributor to free leadership e-resources at www.sharpeningleaders.com.

Learn more about Steve at www.steveabrown.com.

About Arrow Leadership

For over twenty years, the Arrow Leadership Program has been used by God to profoundly shape the hearts, lives and leadership of Christian leaders in North America and beyond. Arrow's focus is to develop Christlike servant leaders who are "led more by Jesus, lead more like Jesus and lead more to Jesus."

The Arrow Leadership Program has two distinct streams:

Emerging Stream: An 18-month transformational experience for ministry leaders (25–40) serving in church or parachurch ministry. The highly personalized and intentional approach accelerates growth and leverages impact for ministry leaders who are seeking to deepen and increase their leadership capacity in three key areas: calling, character and competency.

Executive Stream: Carefully crafted for Christian leaders (any age) serving in executive leadership roles, this 15-month experience focuses on personal, team and organizational leadership.

To learn more, please visit: www.arrowleadership.org.